1981

The Developing Child

Recent decades have witnessed unprecedented advances in research on human development. Each book in The Developing Child series reflects the importance of this research as a resource for enhancing children's well-being. It is the purpose of the series to make this resource available to that increasingly large number of people who are responsible for raising a new generation. We hope that these books will provide rich and useful information for parents, educators, child-care professionals, students of developmental psychology, and all others concerned with childhood.

Jerome Bruner, University of Oxford
Michael Cole, Rockefeller University
Barbara Lloyd, University of Sussex
Series Editors

The Developing Child Series

Mental Retardation

Robert B. Edgerton

Harvard University Press
Cambridge, Massachusetts
1979

Library of Congress Cataloging in Publication Data

Edgerton, Robert B   1931-
   Mental retardation.

   (The Developing child)
   Bibliography: p.
   Includes index.
   1. Mentally handicapped children.   2. Mentally
handicapped.   I. Title.   II. Series.
[DNLM: 1. Mental retardation. WS107.3 E23m]
HV891.E34   1979   362.3   78-27199
ISBN 0-674-56885-0
ISBN 0-674-56886-9 pbk.

For Christine

Acknowledgments

I wish to acknowledge the support provided by the National Institute of Child Health and Human Development, Public Health Service Grant No. HD 04612, and the Mental Retardation Research Center, University of California, Los Angeles, Grant No. HD 05540-02. I am grateful to Robert S. Sparkes for providing me with the Down's syndrome karyotype, and to Patti S. Hartmann for her diligent research assistance. My thanks go to Lupe Montaño for typing various versions of this book with her usual good humor and skill.

Contents

Credits

Mental Retardation

1 / What Is Mental Retardation?

Despite the seemingly awesome hazards that menace the developing child, very few children are born with serious defects, and the vast majority of children who are healthy at birth grow up to become relatively normal adults. Nevertheless, there *are* hazards for the developing child, and not all children will grow up to be normal. Some of these hazards are biological, others environmental. Today, as many as three out of every one hundred children born in the United States and Great Britain will be diagnosed as mentally retarded at some time in their lives. Some 20 to 25 percent of these children will be so severely retarded that their condition will be diagnosed at birth or in infancy. The majority of mentally retarded children will have milder degrees of intellectual impairment, and most of these children will not be diagnosed as retarded until they enter school. Some may not actually be retarded at all; others may lose the diagnosis after they become adults. Nevertheless, in terms of the numbers of children affected, mental retardation is the most handicapping of all childhood disorders. (It is also an immensely costly problem. Depending on how one computes direct and indirect costs, estimates of the annual cost of mental retardation in the United States in 1978 ranged between 5 and 10 billion dollars.)

The term "mental retardation" is used to refer to a variety of physical and mental conditions. Retarded persons vary widely in intellectual ability, from the profoundly retarded who may possess no speech and no testable IQ, and who must live vegetative lives under continual medical supervision, to the mildly retarded, many of whom appear to have perfectly normal intellectual ability until confronted by the tasks of mathematics or reading. Some retarded persons also have disabling physical handicaps, but many have none. Some have severe emotional problems, but others are remarkably well adjusted. Some will require protective care throughout their lives, but others will learn to live independently as adults.

Such a diversity of conditions came to be lumped together under the category of "mental retardation" because all such people are thought to suffer from an intellectual deficiency that significantly impairs their ability to become fully competent and independent members of society. The most widely used definition of mental retardation in this country was published in 1977 by the American Association on Mental Deficiency (AAMD): "Mental retardation refers to significantly subaverage general intellectual functioning existing concurrently with deficits in adaptive behavior, and manifested during the developmental period" (the upper age of the developmental period is set at eighteen).[1] The most common British definition, based on the Mental Health Act of 1959, refers to severe subnormality (rather than mental retardation), which is described as "a state of arrested or incomplete development of mind which includes subnormality of intelligence and is of such a nature and degree that the patient is incapable of leading an independent life or of guarding himself against serious exploitation, or will be incapable when of an age to do so." Less severe retardation is referred to as subnormality, defined as a condition "which includes subnormality of intelligence and is of a nature or degree which requires or is susceptible to medical treatment or other special care or training of the patient."

While it is obvious that neither the American nor the British definition is particularly precise, each refers to below-average intelligence, which is most commonly defined today as an IQ score below 70. The AAMD definition stresses deficient *adaptive behavior*, defined as standards of personal independence and social responsibility expected in a person's age and cultural group. This emphasis is obviously needed in the United States because of the recognition that children or adults from ethnically different backgrounds (say Afro-Americans or Puerto Ricans) or from culturally different or deprived areas (say Appalachia or Indian reservations) may do poorly on IQ tests and yet behave in a manner that is entirely appropriate for the expectations of people in their subculture. Although this degree of cultural pluralism is not as extreme in Great Britain, it is by no means absent, as witness the subaverage IQ test scores of West Indian and Irish children.

TYPES OF RETARDATION

There are systems of classification based on symptoms and others based on causation, but the most widely used classification refers to the severity of the intellectual handicap. In the past an *idiot* was someone with an IQ of less than 30, an *imbecile* had an IQ of 30 to 50, and a *moron* an IQ of 50 to 70. These terms have been replaced throughout much of the English-speaking world by the AAMD system in which there are these categories: mild retardation (IQ 55-69), moderate retardation (IQ 40-54), severe retardation (IQ 25-39), and profound retardation (IQ less than 25). While the World Health Organization has recommended use of the terms *mild subnormality*, *moderate subnormality*, and *severe subnormality*, their proposal has not been widely accepted.

Tests of adaptive behavior have been developed in the United States and are now used in several countries, but they are useful primarily for the classification of the adaptive skills of younger children with IQ's below the level of mild retardation; these scales have not yet replaced the IQ test as the major means of classification.[2] Estimating the adaptive behavior of more mildly retarded people is still largely a matter of judgment.

Although mental retardation includes a great diversity of conditions brought about by many causes, it is practicable to refer to two basic types: clinical and sociocultural. Since the differences between these two types of retardation are so significant, it is important to distinguish between them before we go any further.

In clinical retardation, the degree of intellectual deficit ranges from moderate to profound, that is, less than IQ 55. The diagnosis of clinical retardation is typically made either at birth or in the first few years of life. Moreover, the condition is largely unchanging throughout life. Clinical retardation can usually be shown to have concomitant organic deficits of a neurological, metabolic, or physiological sort. The causes can often be determined, although the condition cannot usually be effectively treated. Even so, the physical, emotional, and intellectual abilities of clinically retarded people are influenced by the kind of care and education they receive. It is important to note that clinically retarded children are born to people of all social classes and ethnic groups. Indeed, clinically retarded children are born to wealthy, well-educated parents almost as often as they are to poor and uneducated ones. Approximately 20 to 25 percent of all retarded children belong to the clinical category.

Sociocultural retardation accounts for the remaining 75-80 percent of retarded individuals. It involves mild intellectual impairment, with IQ's ranging from 55 to 69. The condition is usually not diagnosed until the child enters school, has academic difficulties, and undergoes psychological assessment. There are seldom any marked physical handicaps and laboratory tests for physical abnormalities are usually negative. Such children are most likely to be born to parents who are economically, socially, and educationally disadvantaged. For example, it has been estimated that a child born in an impoverished rural area or in an urban ghetto is fifteen times more likely to be diagnosed mentally retarded than is a child from a middle-class suburban background.[3] Unlike the more severely retarded children of the clinical category, socioculturally retarded children may behave quite acceptably in their everyday lives even though their classroom performances tend to be below average.

Parents of clinically retarded children typically seek treatment and counseling from available medical resources in order to cope with the child's physical and intellectual handicaps. On the other hand, parents of socioculturally retarded children often refuse to accept the label, and some become antagonistic to the school system as well as to the psychological testing that led their child to be called "retarded" and set apart from other children.

The two types of retardation, then, are dramatically different in terms of severity, causes, and the problems they pose for parents, relatives, and society.

2 / Clinical Retardation

It is not always possible to identify a specific biological etiology for a clinically retarded child, but general knowledge of the causes of clinical retardation is improving rapidly. It is not important—or possible—to list here all of the many hundreds of causes. Instead I shall identify only some of the most common factors, before going on to ask what can be done to prevent this condition.

CAUSES

Infections. There are several major diseases that can cause mental retardation in the developing fetus. The most important are toxoplasmosis, syphilis, rubella (German measles), and cytomegalic inclusion disease (a virus related to herpes). Among these only rubella is now reasonably well controlled. For the others there is either no vaccine or no cure. There are also several diseases that produce post-infectious encephalitis, which can cause mental retardation in children: meningitis, rubella, mumps, and chicken pox.

Intoxication. The principal forms of intoxication which affect the developing fetus are toxemia of pregnancy, which is still a major obstetrical problem, maternal phenylketonuria (PKU), hyperbilirubinemia, lead poisoning, and maternal alcoholism.

All of these diseases may harm the developing brain. Thus, a mother with PKU bears children who are mentally retarded even though they do not have PKU. Hyperbilirubinemia is associated with Rh incompatibility (also with sepsis, prematurity, or neo-

7

natal hepatitis). Lead poisoning is an old problem which is now receiving greater attention because of the recognition that even small amounts of lead may cause mental retardation. Heavy maternal consumption of alcohol is also now recognized as a potential threat to the developing fetus.

Clinical retardation may also be caused by trauma as the result of injury to the pregnant mother, perinatal injury through the improper use of forceps in delivery, or postnatal injury to the child from an accident or abuse. Anoxia (lack of oxygen), either at birth from obstetrical difficulties or later in life from injury or near-drowning, may also leave the victim profoundly retarded.

Disorders of Metabolism or Nutrition. There are various metabolic disorders (such as Tay-Sachs disease) which lead to mental retardation, often after a period of degeneration. Mental retardation can also be caused by carbohydrate disorders, such as galactosemia, in which a newborn infant cannot tolerate milk; by amino acid disorders, nucleotide disorders, or mineral disorders (the best known of which is cretinism from a deficiency of a thyroid hormone); and by severe malnutrition, which can substantially impair cognitive development. There are also various forms of gross brain disease and cranial malformation, as well as a host of gestational disorders involving such factors as premature birth, low birth weight, or placental dysfunction, which in combination with a child's later social and educational experience may lead to mental retardation.

Genetic Anomalies. Finally, there are many genetic anomalies that produce clinical retardation in varying degrees of severity. The best known of these, Down's syndrome, usually stems from an abnormal number of chromosomes, as in Turner's syndrome, Klinefelter's syndrome, and several others. Perhaps 80 percent of the known genetic causes of mental retardation are attributable to chromosomal anomalies, but clinical retardation can also result from single gene mutations, such as those seen in PKU, Tay-Sachs disease, metachromatic leukodystrophy, Von Recklinghausen's disease, and various forms of microcephaly and hydrocephalus.

Even this partial and sketchy introduction to the causes of

clinical retardation must seem both a very long and a very dismal litany indeed. And few parents will be equipped to understand how or why these afflictions might affect their child. The most vital question, then, is what can be done to prevent clinical retardation?

GENETIC COUNSELING

The best insurance against clinical retardation now available is genetic counseling. It provides an individual, couple, or family with specific information concerning the chances of their child's inheriting a particular genetic disease that produces retardation, as well as the nature of the disease and the possibility of prevention or treatment. Genetic counseling begins with the collection of a detailed family history or genealogy, which includes information on the couple's former marriages, family illnesses, and abortions. A history is also taken of the present or planned pregnancy which brought the patient to the clinic. Finally a physician carries out a complete physical examination.

Specific diagnostic techniques include metabolic screening, in which an amino acid chromatogram is usually routine with all patients. Urinary screening is advisable when there is more than one retarded child in a family. Many states now require screenings by law to prevent PKU, among other diseases. Chromosome analysis based on a simple blood test is also valuable and may permit the accurate identification of an abnormal chromosome. But perhaps the most important development in genetic counseling is amniocentesis.

Amniocentesis, which was first developed in 1966, is a relatively simple outpatient procedure that usually takes only a few minutes to carry out and rarely causes the patient discomfort. The procedure is usually carried out at fourteen to sixteen weeks during pregnancy. Under a local anesthetic, a needle about the same size as that used for a penicillin injection is introduced through the abdominal and uterine walls into the amniotic fluid sac. A small amount (about 20 ml) of fluid is removed and used for an analysis of the fetal chromosomes. Because the fetal cells from the amniotic fluid must grow in a special nutrient medium, this chromosome analysis usually takes three to four weeks; metabolic studies require a larger number of cells and a longer time to complete. The main risk of the procedure is that the fetus will abort, but that occurs in substantially less than 1 percent of the cases. Many genetic screening centers recommend that a newer procedure, ultrasound screening of the uterus, should precede amniocentesis in order to ascertain the position of the fetus and thereby reduce risk. This nonsurgical procedure can be used routinely to locate the fetus, measure it, determine gestational age, and so on. It can also be used in the detection of various congenital malformations that may be related to mental retardation.

Except in rare cases, amniocentesis permits a precise determination of risk (from 0 percent to 100 percent) for a specific form of genetic abnormality. While the test can determine whether the baby will suffer from Down's syndrome, Tay-Sachs disease, or another genetic disorder, it cannot determine whether the baby will be biologically "normal" in all respects. Still amniocentesis has enormous value in the prevention of clinical retardation. For example, Down's syndrome (formerly known as Mongolism) is one of the most common types of clinical retardation. Almost 95 percent of all Down's births are due to trisomy 21 (an anomaly of chromosome number 21). While the incidence of trisomy 21 is approximately 1 in 600 births (not a very great risk), the risk increases with the age of the mother. For mothers aged twenty, the risk is 1 in 2000, but by the age of thirty-five the risk is 1 in 300, and by age forty-five it may be as great as 1 in 16. To place this risk factor in another perspective, mothers over thirty-five years of age produce only 7 percent of all live births in the United States, but these same mothers contribute close to 30 percent of all the Down's children born here each year.

It is clear, then, that if all mothers over thirty-five were to have their pregnancies monitored by amniocentesis, it would be possible to identify Down's syndrome prenatally in a great many pregnancies. Of course, if all mothers were so monitored, *all* Down's pregnancies could be identified, although this course is not now recommended since the risk factor in younger mothers is so low and since the available facilities are quite limited. The expense of amniocentesis is also a consideration, since the procedure costs about $500. We should also note that identifying a Down's pregnancy by amniocentesis does not mean that therapeutic abortion would necessarily follow. Genetic counseling involves a full explanation of the physical and mental characteristics of a Down's child. Parents are informed about the availability of local service agencies and about the need for follow-up medical care. The developmental disabilities of Down's children are explained in view of their possible impact on the family, especially on normal siblings. After all this information has been discussed, the decision to continue the pregnancy or to terminate it remains with the parents.

Many children with inborn errors of metabolism usually appear to be perfectly normal at birth, only to develop clinical retardation later in childhood. Fortunately, many of these disorders can now be identified by genetic screening and counseling. One condition that can be readily prevented is PKU, which occurs once in every 10,000 births or so. Most states require screening of all newborns for PKU, and many affected children have been identified as a result. Untreated PKU children are frequently (but not always) mentally retarded. Treatment involves a diet low in phenylalanine (the amino acid responsible for PKU), which is usually continued until five years of age and sometimes longer. Because the disease cannot be detected in amniotic fluid cells, an affected fetus cannot be identified prenatally. Thus there is a pressing need for the screening of newborns and for counseling those who may be PKU carriers (all children of an affected individual will be PKU carriers).

A recent and most important development is the capability of detecting congenital hypothyroidism (cretinism), a condition that occurs once in every 6000 births. Because cretinism develops slowly over the first six months of life, there is often delayed diagnosis and treatment. As is the case with PKU, the longer the condition is untreated (some authorities believe that treatment must begin by the age of three months), the greater the risk of impaired physical and intellectual development. Thanks to a simple blood sampling technique developed in Canada in 1974, cretinism can now be detected and treated in newborns.

Tay-Sachs disease is another genetic disorder that could be prevented by genetic counseling. The disease results from the absence of a particular enzyme (hexoseaminidase-A); as a result, the body cannot assimilate certain fats. Although an affected child often appears normal at birth, the disease usually appears during the first year of life, beginning with a deterioration of motor ability and voluntary movement. As the disease progresses, the child develops severe retardation, blindness, and convulsions. Death usually occurs by the fourth year of life. This ghastly affliction is especially common among Ashkenazi Jews (principally from Central and Eastern Europe) where 1 out of 30 persons is a carrier as opposed to 1 in 300 in other ethnic groups. Fortunately there is now a simple blood test that permits identification of genetic carriers of Tay-Sachs disease before pregnancy. When both parents are carriers, there is a 25 percent risk that their child will be affected. Should such parents nevertheless wish to have a child, amniocentesis can be utilized to determine the presence of hexoseaminidase-A in the amniotic fluid cells. If this identification is positive, the fetus will be aborted.

Who should consider genetic counseling or amniocentesis? Each family should pose that question to a physician, but as a rule of thumb, amniocentesis is indicated when the mother is over thirty-five years of age; when either parent has had a Down's child previously, is a suspected carrier of a genetic anomaly, or has had a previous child with a chromosome abnormality or multiple malformations; or when a woman has had multiple miscarriages for no apparent reason.[1]

As facilities for genetic counseling and amniocentesis expand, it will be possible to prevent the occurrence of many serious forms of clinical retardation. It is probable that fewer than 5 percent of the families of clinically retarded children in the United States received genetic counseling. Although it will be expensive to expand genetic counseling facilities, it is well to keep in mind the high cost of caring for a retarded child in a hospital setting, and when the human cost to the affected child and the family are considered, it is obvious that counseling services must be made far more widely available. To place this warning in another perspective, a recent survey in northern England reported that 42 percent of all childhood deaths in hospitals were due to conditions that were largely genetically determined.[2]

MATERNAL INFECTION

In addition to genetic screening and counseling, there are other precautions that should be taken by concerned parents. One major concern is maternal infection. Some dangerous infections, such as rubella (German measles), can cause severe damage to the unborn child. Perhaps because rubella was so long thought of as a mild childhood disease and because it is often asymptomatic in adults, it was not until 1941 that it was discovered that maternal infection by rubella—even when it is asymptomatic—can cause serious fetal damage, including among other things blindness, deafness, heart disease, and mental retardation. When the mother becomes infected during the first trimester of pregnancy, the damage to the fetus is most severe. Since an effective vaccine against rubella has been available since 1969, there is little danger of an epidemic of rubella like the one in the early 1960s, which killed or severely damaged over 50,000 children in the United States.

While most women today presumably know about the danger of rubella and recognize the need for vaccination, other dangerous diseases may be unheard of even by college-educated parents. For example, toxoplasmosis is an infectious disease that can cause severe clinical retardation (often in the form of hydrocephalus). Since the disease affects one baby in every 1000 births, it is hardly a rare disorder. The disease often has flu-like symptoms, but it may produce no symptoms at all in a pregnant woman and still affect her unborn child. Toxoplasmosis is caused by a parasite that is transmitted in rare or raw meat or in the feces of infected house cats. Like rubella, the severity of the damage depends on the stage of pregnancy, and about half the time, the organisms that have infected the mother do not pass through the placenta to infect the fetus. In some cases, the disease remains dormant in an affected child until much later in life (some victims remain normal until their twenties or even later). There is still no cure for toxoplasmosis, but a blood test is now available which can determine even before pregnancy whether a woman has had the disease and is immune. Simple precautions can also be taken. Pregnant women should eat well-cooked meat and stay away from the litter boxes of cats.

Similarly, while the dangers of congenital syphilis (which include mental retardation) are reasonably well known, and while there are readily available blood tests for its diagnosis as well as a simple and effective treatment, another venereal disease is twice as common as syphilis in the United States and its dangers are relatively unknown. Herpes Simplex Virus 2 (HSV-2) can be deadly to unborn and newborn children and, as yet, the disease is incurable. In some cases, the child is born already infected with the virus, but in most cases the infection is transmitted as the newborn infant passes through the infected birth canal. The disease has a very high mortality rate for infants (upwards of 75 percent) and of those who survive, as many as 75 percent will suffer some neurological damage, often clinical retardation. Since many women are not aware that they are infected by HSV-2, and others regard it as an insignificant if unpleasant affliction, the disease may easily go undetected until birth. This is particularly unfortunate because, when HSV-2 is diagnosed and carefully monitored, the chances of transmitting the disease to the newborn child can be greatly lessened. The most common method now in use involves Caesarian section to avoid the infection in the birth canal and isolation of the baby from its mother for a number of days until the mother is free of active viral infection.

There are many other pre- and postpartum diseases that can produce clinical mental retardation, including cytomegalic inclusion disease, which causes at least 4000 severely retarded births each year in the United States. An informed and concerned mother should not only seek competent medical care once she thinks she is pregnant, but ideally she should do so as soon as she contemplates having a child.

DRUGS AND ALCOHOL

The horror of the more than 3600 "thalidomide babies" born in Europe in the 1960s made much of the world aware of what has long been recognized in medicine—many substances interfere with normal fetal development. These include coagulants (such as Warfarin), anticonvulsants (Dilantin, trimethadione, paramethadione), steroids, quinine, hormones, common antihistamines and antibiotics, as well as a variety of narcotics including tobacco and alcohol. While the safe use of most of these substances requires the advice of a physician, some, like alcohol, have only recently been recognized as serious dangers, and the wise use of these substances remains largely in the hands of the mother herself. Since alcohol is so great a part of Euro-American society and since the dangers of maternal drinking have so long gone unrecognized, let us use alcohol to illustrate the more general problem of taking drugs and medication during pregnancy.

Classical Greek and Roman mythology and medicine suggested that heavy drinking by the mother at the time of conception could lead to fetal damage, a view that at one time or another has been expressed in many of the world's drinking cultures. In more recent history, when England removed its restrictions on distilled alcoholic beverages, inexpensive gin flooded the country from 1720 to 1750, creating the infamous "gin epidemic" and providing Hogarth with material for his art. During those years birth rates dropped, and childhood mortality rose sharply. As early as 1726, the College of Physicians petitioned Parliament for control of the distilling trade, referring to gin as the cause of weak and feebleminded children. Indeed, throughout the nineteenth century in Britain and the United States there were countless medical observations linking parental alcoholism with all sorts of infant enfeeblement, including mental retardation. In the twentieth century, however, such dire pronouncements were gradually dismissed as unsupported alarmism deriving in large part from temperance thinking.

So complete was the rejection of alcohol as the cause of fetal development deficiency that it was not until 1973 that the Fetal Alcohol Syndrome (FAS) was "discovered" by scientists.[3] Because of interference with cellular metabolism, this syndrome involves various growth deficiencies, cranial and facial deformities, limb defects, and mental retardation. The average IQ of FAS children is 60 to 65, but some are more severely retarded. There are thought to be 1500 FAS children born each year in the United States. Recent research throughout Europe and the Soviet Union confirms the existence of FAS, although it still is not certain to what extent the fetal damage comes from chronic drinking by the mother as opposed to occasional binge drinking. There is some reason to suspect that both are involved, with binge drinking probably being most dangerous during the twelfth to eighteenth gestational weeks, the period when multiplication of brain cells in the fetus is most rapid.

While there is no evidence to link the father's drinking to developmental defects in the fetus, it now seems clear that maternal drinking places the fetus at considerable risk. Based on available research, much of it with animals, the National Institute of Alcohol Abuse and Alcoholism warned that any mother who has six or more drinks of alcohol per day is placing her unborn child at significant risk of FAS, including mental retardation of "35 to 40 IQ points below average." In fact, the institute believes that risk is involved in a pregnant woman who has even two drinks a day, stating that the risk rises to at least a 50 percent likelihood of producing a retarded child if the woman has ten drinks a day. Still more recent research in the United States has confirmed that two drinks a day, especially in the month just *prior* to the recognition of pregnancy, puts the fetus at considerable risk of FAS, perhaps as much as 10 percent. Since a woman may not be aware that she is pregnant for two or more weeks after conception, it is clear that the risk of alcohol consumption is a real one for women who are not using effective means of birth control.[4] The risks of binge drinking in this period before pregnancy are still not known.

So serious is the risk of maternal drinking now considered to be that the National Institute of Alcohol Abuse and Alcoholism issued a public warning in the summer of 1977, despite the fact that the results of several large-scale research projects then underway were not yet available, and in November of 1977 the Food and Drug Administration asked the Bureau of Alcohol, Tobacco, and Firearms to require labels on alcoholic beverages warning women that heavy drinking during pregnancy may cause birth defects.

While definitive research has not yet been reported, and some scientists are therefore skeptical, there can be no doubt that maternal alcoholism can produce mental retardation. The prudent course for pregnant women and women who are contemplating pregnancy would appear to be that of severely limiting their intake of alcohol, and consulting their doctors about all other drugs and medications.

OTHER PREVENTABLE CAUSES OF RETARDATION

Among many other causes of clinical mental retardation, a few warrant particular mention. Many children each year become mentally retarded as a result of brain damage from accidents or child abuse. Indeed in the United States in 1973 the leading cause of death of children aged one to four was accidents, with car accidents a close second. Parents can guard against the latter by using seatbelts in their cars and by requiring safety headgear for children on bicycles and on the increasingly popular, and dangerous, skateboards. Public recognition that child abuse is widespread and that defenseless children are being battered, sometimes with resulting permanent brain damage, may also bring about a reduction in this particularly tragic source of mental retardation.

Radiation can also lead to mental retardation either by causing a mutation before conception or by damaging the fetus during its development; this happened to pregnant women as a result of the nuclear bomb explosions at Hiroshima and Nagasaki. Common results of excessive radiation are microcephaly, hydrocephalus, spina bifida, and cleft palate. Since what constitutes "excessive" radiation is not yet known, pregnant women can only be urged—even more than the rest of us—to avoid x-rays and sources of industrial radiation.

Various environmental poisons may also cause mental retardation. Of these, the most widespread and dangerous is lead. In my discussion of sociocultural retardation I shall consider lead poisoning more fully, but I should note here that severe lead poisoning can be caused by pica, a disease characterized by habitual and sometimes compulsive eating of nonfood substances such as plaster, paint, clay, dirt, newspapers, cigarette butts, string, laundry starch, and so on. Authorities differ regarding the causes of pica, some attributing it to nutritional deficiencies, others to emotional factors. Regardless of the cause, it is important for parents to keep in mind that lead dust is common in many cities, as is lead-based paint or plaster in older buildings. The daily ingestion of only a few flakes of lead-based paint for two or three months can be sufficient to bring about a lethal dose of lead poisoning in small children. Many children who survive lead poisoning suffer permanent, severe retardation.

To summarize, there are various steps that can be taken to prevent mental retardation. Before conception parents can seek genetic counseling to determine the genetic risk of having a retarded child; parents can time and space pregnancies, and assure that the mother is receiving adequate nutrition; the mother should also seek full immunization. During pregnancy, care must be taken to protect mother and fetus against infection, to continue proper nutrition, to avoid alcohol and other drugs, and to allow continuous medical monitoring of the pregnancy. When appropriate, amniocentesis should include screening for conditions that cause mental retardation, protection of Rh-negative mothers with gamma globulin within seventy-two hours of delivery, and intensive care of infants born prematurely or ill. Finally, in early childhood proper nutrition should be maintained for the child and the nursing mother; metabolic conditions should receive proper dietary management; and environmental hazards such as lead should be removed or avoided. And, always, a stimulating social and educational setting should be provided for clinically retarded children. Even severely retarded children may improve greatly in response to a favorable social, emotional, and intellectual environment.

3 / If Prevention Fails

Despite advances in the prevention of mental retardation, many thousands of clinically retarded children are born each year. Some, usually the most profoundly retarded, will not survive infancy, but the majority will live many years and many will have a normal life expectancy. What can be done to care for, treat, and educate these children? Owing to the great diversity of conditions involved, it is difficult to generalize about clinical retardation. Therefore, let us first consider the most common and best understood form—Down's syndrome—which accounts for about 25 percent of the clinically retarded. Approximately one in every thousand children born will have this condition.

THE DIAGNOSIS

Because of the characteristic physical appearance of a Down's syndrome infant, a doctor or nurse can diagnose the condition at birth 85 to 90 percent of the time. In a few cases, the characteristic facial appearance, lack of muscular tone, and fingerprint and skin patterns of a Down's infant are so minimal that cytogenetic study must be conducted before a diagnosis can be confirmed. But in most cases, the diagnosis is made and presented to the parents shortly after birth.

How the physician first presents the diagnosis to the parents not only has immense emotional impact at that moment—it may have lasting effects as well. The following examples convey the shock and the confusion of these initial encounters with the physician:

And then the doctor came in and he drew the curtains around my cubicle and I thought, oh no, you know. And he told me the baby was born completely healthy, but he's not completely normal. And I looked at him and I said, he's mongoloid. And I've never seen a mongoloid baby before in my life, but all of a sudden the flat features, the thrusting of the tongue, you know, just kind of hit me in the face. And that poor doctor couldn't bring himself to say the word. He said, it shouldn't have happened to you, not to your age bracket.[1]

But sometimes the diagnosis is delayed:

Well, I can tell you one thing—we did not know at birth that Christopher was mongoloid. We did not know until he was six months old. And it seemed that when he was born he very definitely had mongoloid features . . . the doctor had told my husband this, but we didn't know what it meant. I really didn't know what a mongoloid child was. And my husband said, oh the doctor said there might be something wrong with his features. And when the doctor came in I asked him and he said, oh no, no problem, he'll be perfectly all right . . . But then when he was 6 months old, they told us of the possibility that he might be mongoloid. And of course, we both completely went to pieces. After having three other children you'd have thought we'd know more about it. We didn't. I didn't know what a mongoloid child was . . . So we immediately went to the library and got all the books that we could on the subject. And they were all old, old stuff and threw us into a complete tizzy. We felt that he may never walk. He had already rolled over, and his development was somewhat normal. And we thought we might have just a vegetable. We both went into just a complete mental thing which I think I am sort of coming out of now, but my husband isn't. He is not aware of this, but he really isn't. He has never been the same since . . . We got the good news Christmas Eve day that he was a mongoloid.[2]

The following example, from a city in the eastern United States, illustrates the tendency of many physicians to treat Down's children as hopeless and to recommend that they be institutionalized.

The very next day after his birth they told me that he was a mongoloid and that there was nothing to do except to put him in an institution. On the eighth day two other doctors, one in the afternoon and one in the evening, examined David and confirmed the diagnosis. The one in the afternoon said, "He's going to be retarded all his life and there's nothing you can do about it." The one in the evening said, "He has all the symptoms of mongolism and there is nothing left for you to do but put him in an institution." The other doctor gave me no encouragement whatsoever. It was the blunt curtness of his response to my questions that hurt. When I would ask questions like, "When will he sit up?" he would reply shortly, "I don't know if he'll ever sit up." It was that sort of thing that got me. When I took David in for his first six-week check-up, the pediatrician never told me how he was progressing or expressed interest. He merely undressed him, looked at him, said he'd always be sickly and susceptible to pneumonia.[3]

E. R. Kramm studied fifty families that had children with Down's syndrome and found that forty-four families had been advised to seek institutional placement at the time they were first told of the diagnosis, and thirty-one of these were told to do so immediately. Benjamin Spock recalls his own experience in dealing with parents:

When I made the diagnosis of mongolism in a newborn baby, I (like most pediatricians at that time) believed that I was giving the best possible help to the parents by advising them, if they could afford it, to place him at once in a nursing home, preferably without ever seeing him. This was on the theory that then they would not become painfully attached to him, and would be better able to provide a cheerful atmosphere and plenty of attention to their subsequent children. As if anguish and guilt could be solved by trying to forget.[4]

Most physicians now agree that the diagnosis should be conveyed to the parents as early as possible, adding that the doctor should be sympathetic to the parents and answer all their questions fully but should not give false encouragement or too much direct advice concerning institutional placement. However, as recent research has shown, pediatricians are still influenced by their own values, religious convictions, and even age, with older physicians being more likely than younger ones to recommend that parents institutionalize their clinically retarded child.[5]

THE CAUSES OF DOWN'S SYNDROME

Down's syndrome was identified in 1866 by the English physician Langdon Down who called the disorder "Mongolism" because he thought that Down's syndrome children resembled Asians. Because of the negative racial connotations of the term and its inaccuracy as a physical comparison (the Chinese, for example, are able to distinguish Down's syndrome children from normal children as easily as the British can), mongolism has been replaced by the term "Down's syndrome." About 95 percent of Down's births are caused by an extra chromosome (trisomy-21). Normally, of course, humans have forty-six chromosomes joined together in twenty-three pairs, but in Down's syndrome there is an extra number-21 chromosome, giving such individuals a total of forty-seven (see the karyotype reproduced here).

The remaining cases of Down's syndrome are caused by mosaicism or translocation. Mosaicism results when faulty chromosomal distribution occurs in the developing embryo after fertilization. Some experts believe that mosaicism is important to

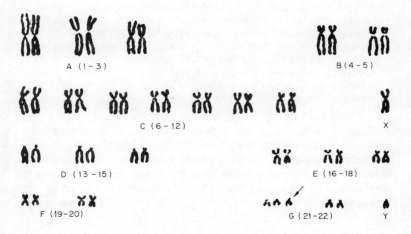

A (1-3)   B (4-5)

C (6-12)   X

D (13-15)   E (16-18)

F (19-20)   G (21-22)   Y

identify since such people may have more nearly normal intellectual abilities than will persons with trisomy-21. In translocation, all or a part of a chromosome becomes attached to all or a part of another chromosome, forming a single "translocation" chromosome. There is considerable risk that future children of the parents of a translocation Down's child will also be affected, and so early identification is important here, too.

Years ago it was thought that "mongolism" was a throwback to a more primitive racial type or even to the orangutan. As these theories found their final resting places, it was noticed that the mothers of many mongoloid children were of advanced age. This observation led to various theories about maternal problems, such as exhaustion, and anxiety. Such theories raised illusory hopes that improved maternal care could eliminate the disease. Although the genetic basis of Down's syndrome is now known, the specific causes of these anomalies have still not been identified. It is suspected that aging of the ovum, genetic predisposition, and environmental factors may be implicated.

Since 1977 evidence has been presented showing that the cause of trisomy-21 is not always a fault in the mother's ovum. In research conducted at the University of Oregon by R. Magenis and his colleagues, new techniques for examining chromosomes were used to determine whether the father or mother contributed the extra number-21 chromosome that had led to their child's Down's syndrome condition.[6] In more than 20 percent of the cases studied, the father's sperm, not the mother's ovum, contained the extra chromosome. It is not yet known whether the age of the father is related to the likelihood that he will contribute the extra chromosome.

PHYSICAL SIGNS

Although the diagnostic signs of Down's syndrome vary somewhat from one case to the next, just as they change with age, the physical appearances of those with the syndrome are remarkably alike. It should be noted, however, that neither the number nor the kind of physical signs present is related to IQ or to intellectual impairment. Most of the signs are meaningful only as aids to diagnosis. These include poor muscle tone; small head size; a small nose that in profile appears to be flat; slanting eyes with epicanthal folds; small ears, sometimes with the helix (upper rim) folded over; a protruding and fissured tongue; teeth that erupt late and are abnormally placed or shaped; a short broad neck; small square hands with short fingers, a distinctive palm crease and fingerprints (loops instead of whorls); mottled dry skin; and sparse, fine, and straight hair. The brains and therefore the skulls are quite small, although because of the smaller stature of Down's syndrome people this may not be immediately apparent. Thus Down's children at the age of fifteen have a head size comparable to a normal child aged two and a half.

DEVELOPMENT AND HEALTH

Down's syndrome children have birth weights in the low normal range, but later in life they may have problems with obesity. Birth length is also normal; adult stature is short (on the average 5 feet for men; 4 feet 7 inches for women), but it has been increasing in recent years, probably as a result of improved control of serious infections and better nutrition. Many Down's children have heart defects, malfunctioning of the lower intestine, and a susceptibility to respiratory infection. About 1 percent develop leukemia. In 1929 their life expectancy was only nine years; in 1949 it had improved to twelve years and by 1959 it was eighteen years. Today, some 20 to 30 percent of Down's babies do not survive the first few years, but those who do survive can be expected to live to the sixth or even seventh decade of life.

In the first six months of life, motor development is relatively normal. Thereafter such tasks as dressing, eating, and other self-care skills are developed from one to two years behind the normal population. The greatest developmental lag involves the acquisition of speech, which in most cases is delayed beyond the normal rate by a year or more. When speech does develop (often between the fourth and sixth years) the language used will be simple and difficult to understand. The ability of Down's children to understand speech is much closer to normal than is their ability to speak themselves.

In adolescence, sexual development is usually delayed or incomplete. Males have small genitalia and appear never to be fertile. Females menstruate at the average age, and a few Down's women have reproduced; about half of their offspring have had the syndrome. The aging process differs somewhat from the normal one, particularly in the progressive dryness and coarseness of the skin, the recession of the gums, and various changes in the brain normally associated with senility.

MENTAL DEVELOPMENT

Most Down's children have tested IQs that range from 35 to 54. A few are more severely retarded and some are only mildly retarded. This considerable range in intellectual impairment has important implications for parents. First, Down's children whose syndrome is due to mosaicism typically have higher IQs than those found in children with trisomy-21. Thus, mosaic children have IQs that average near 70 and a few have normal intelligence.[7] In planning for the life of their children, then, parents should have the genetic basis of the child determined. However, it must be emphasized that *all* Down's children, like normal children, respond to and benefit from a stimulating environment. For example, Down's children who have been raised in institutions have IQs substantially lower than those of children raised at home. Although Down's children do have limitations on their intellectual attainments, not all such individuals are fated to remain at a low intellectual level. Before considering what parents might do to encourage the intellectual and personal growth of their Down's children, it is useful to discuss the intellectual and psychological characteristics of these children.

As noted before, Down's syndrome children are markedly deficient in the development of language, particularly in the abstract and complex uses of language. There is also evidence that they are deficient in higher-order intellectual tasks involving abstraction. These deficits may be related to the perceptual deficits which such children also suffer. However, Down's syndrome people are more nearly normal in rote learning, concrete language use, and visual motor skills. These skills relate to the development of social competence, and in this area Down's syndrome people do far better than they do in cognitive development or in school tasks. Down's adults only rarely live independently, but many can learn to behave in socially appropriate ways and to work productively with the supervision of a parent, friend, or caregiver.

Language, or at least the ability to articulate speech, has been reported to be more affected in Down's syndrome than in any other condition associated with mental retardation. It is often painfully difficult to understand the speech of Down's people. However, parents and siblings who have years of experience in listening to the speech of a Down's child can learn to understand very well. This suggests, as one recent study points out, that the garbled speech of such a child does not accurately reflect his communicative abilities. Research by D. R. Price-Williams and S. Sabsay shows that even severely retarded Down's syndrome individuals may be capable of participating in well-structured, successful communicative interactions, in spite of their articulatory deficits. Their study also suggests that learning sign language may be of particular benefit for individuals with severe speech problems.[8]

After providing this review of the characteristics of Down's syndrome people, I must add an important corrective: these people, whether children or adults, are by no means all alike. They differ in IQ from profound to mild retardation, and they differ greatly in the age at which they learn to sit, walk, and speak, much *more* so in fact than is the case in any group of normal children. The fact that a child has Down's syndrome says far less than is generally believed about the intellectual, social, or personal development of that child. For example, it has long been thought (and written) that Down's children are remarkably tractable, friendly, happy, affectionate, and lovable. Recent research indicates that this stereotype is far from the truth: Down's children appear to have the same range of personality attributes—including orneriness—as other children, both normal and retarded. It is vital that parents of a Down's child realize that, although the chromosomal aberration sets limits on development, within these limits it is possible for the child to attain considerable personal and intellectual growth, in his own uniquely individual way.

The clearest evidence that the potential of Down's syndrome persons for intellectual and social growth can be influenced by the environment comes from the well-established research finding that Down's children raised in institutions are substantially less competent than children raised by their parents. There is also evidence to suggest that the quality of life available in the parental home can affect the health and development of the Down's child. Thus while the research evidence is not yet clear-cut, it appears to be the case that a stimulating home environment leads to improved development in Down's children. Furthermore, some preschool programs have reported striking gains in intellectual growth and verbal ability for these children. There is every reason to believe that Down's children, like normal children, respond well to a positive, stimulating environment. Although the once popular biochemical and dietary therapies, including massive doses of vitamins, have failed to improve development, early and intensive stimulation of the child's environment does hold promise.[9]

In this regard, it is worth consulting the diaries of two Down's syndrome men—one British, one American—who were brought up by devoted, sensitive, and educated parents. The abilities of these two men to appreciate life and participate in it should make it apparent to any reader that it is indeed possible to enrich the lives of Down's people. For example, both developed remarkable, almost normal, verbal skills, including the regular use of wry and sarcastic humor. Their comments on life around them were seldom very abstract or highly introspective, but they were often interesting and perceptive. Consider this diary entry from Paul Scott, the American, when at age twenty-one he accompanied his father to the Soviet Union. Amid complaints about Russian money, poverty, and the "deplorable" transportation facilities in Moscow, Paul was struck by the role played by Soviet women:

> Many women in Russia are manually employed. Back from the zoo, the train was run by women conductors, and switch tenders are women, animal feeders in the zoo women, and they are also boot blacks . . . Women wait and cook food in railroad depots, the general employment of women in manual work is to let men enter the enormous Russian military service.[10]

Paul's British counterpart, Nigel Hunt, not only recorded his many impressions of life but typed them as well. The following comment about Henry VIII after a trip to Hampton Court is a good example of his puckish wit: "We came into another gallery and that was Queen Anne's room who old 'Enery' called Anne Boleyn, and how nice of him to look after her!"[11] Nigel's schoolmaster father appended this concluding note to his son's autobiography in an effort to convince parents not to give up hope for their Down's syndrome children even if they are trisomy-21 as Nigel was:

> Before Nigel was five, I was summoned to the senior officer concerned with mental affairs (in a certain county). My wife and Nigel and I went to see this "expert," who was to help decide our child's fate.
> The first thing the good lady said to us—in Nigel's hearing, of course—was, "Oh, yes, a little mongoloid. Quite ineducable. Do you want him put away?"
> Had we been more easily impressed by "experts," we might have said, "Yes."[12]

Mr. Hunt goes on to give the following emphatic message to the parents of Down's children: "Mongoloids can learn and go on learning if they are given encouragement."

This optimistic view is supported by recent research which indicates that there is now a clear possibility—perhaps as great as 50 percent—that even a trisomy-21 Down's child is educable (in psychometric terms, can achieve an IQ above 50). It is also clear that traditional psychometric measures of intelligence in Down's children are far too limiting. Emerging research on early educational programs clearly suggests that the traditional psychometric intelligence of Down's children can be increased, but other, nontraditional measures of "practical" or "social" intelligence indicate that many Down's syndrome people possess the intelligence necessary to live far more normal lives than we have previously imagined.

4 / Caring for the Clinically Retarded

Any parent who undertakes the task of raising any child will require a great deal of strength, patience, understanding, not to mention good humor and luck. When the child is mentally retarded, however, all these qualities and more are required. Such a child frequently has physical handicaps in addition to the mental ones; as a consequence, families may have to make special arrangements for his physical well-being and training as well as his needs for love and companionship. And then there are the problems that parents face alone, the problems of broken dreams for their child, and the fears and guilts that relate to their own lives and hopes. Added to all of these problems are the tensions created by the retarded child's behavior itself, by his handicap in communications, as well as by the financial and practical problems such a child brings to any family. In addition, there are the problems that parents must face with their neighbors, friends, and family. Why did they of all people have such a child? What kind of child is it? What hope can there be for the child? What dangers does the child represent to its brothers and sisters, to the neighbor's children, to the family itself?

Needless to say, each family is unique and its response to a clinically retarded child will differ. Even so, there are some common reactions that families have. Before discussing them we should note very clearly that research into these matters is weak, that we know relatively little about families and the problems they face, and what we do know is based primarily upon limited research with white middle-class families. We *do* know that every family of a clinically retarded child must eventually face the fact that their child is mentally retarded. How this recognition comes about will vary. It may be sudden. It may take place over a period of years. In some cases, as with Down's syndrome children, it may be present at birth. In others, the child may be five or six or even older before the family fully understands that their child is clinically retarded. Once the family does recognize it, they are likely to seek the cause of this tragedy. They do so in part because they hope that they may find some means of curing the retardation or at least preventing it from occurring in any other children they may have in the future. But they will also be concerned with their own burden of responsibility and guilt in bringing such a child into the world. They may feel that they are directly responsible for their child's retardation, even that they have been sent this child by God as a punishment for their sins. Other parents may feel that if they had not done something "wrong" during pregnancy their child would be all right. A retarded child can become the focus of all past wrongs that the parents believe they have committed.

In most instances, with the exception of a few conditions, particularly of Down's syndrome children and phenylketonuria, the parents will learn that it is not possible to identify the specific cause of the retardation. What is more important, except for the syndromes that lead to progressive deterioration, knowing the cause of their child's retardation is of little practical importance. It does not lead to the discovery of a treatment that can "improve" or "cure" the child.

In general, although families spend considerable time searching for the cause, their time would be better spent attempting to evaluate the child's present degree of handicap and planning for his future. Nevertheless, perhaps basing their hopes on what they believe to be the "miraculous cures" of medical science, parents continue to search, hoping they may some day find just the right specialist who has the cure for their child. Many travel from clinic to clinic and doctor to doctor. Others, even more tragically, succumb to quack cures that are expensive, time-consuming, and of no practical value whatsoever. Parents must recognize that, while there are many available therapies involving education and speech, physical development, and help for the deaf and blind, it is very unlikely that any specific *medical* therapy will exist to help their child's mental retardation. Where possible, parents should rely on the expert diagnosis of a physician familiar with mental retardation and be prepared for what is likely to be the truth—that their child's clinical retardation cannot be cured.

Whatever the cause of the child's retardation, it is very likely that the more stable the family, the more harmonious its relationships, the less likely that a retarded child will present serious problems for the adjustment of the family as a whole. Research has indicated that, in families characterized by tension and negative attitudes toward the retarded child, the presence of such a child brings on serious problems in three fourths of such cases. Although the available research is very scanty, clinical evidence suggests that the parents' strengths, their happiness in other areas of their lives, their economic situation and the special needs of their retarded child are among the most significant factors determining what impact the child will have upon the family. Some research indicates that the higher the economic and educational level of the family, the greater is the likelihood that the child will be rejected, perhaps because the retarded child presents too great a contrast with his brothers, sisters, and neighborhood playmates. Families with lower income and less education are sometimes reported to be more accepting of clinically retarded children. In any event, research indicates that the early years of rearing a clinically retarded child are likely to be more stressful than later years, although there is some contrary evidence which we shall discuss later.[1]

Much of the impact of the retarded child falls on the mother. Mothers of retarded children suffer far more psychological stress than do mothers of normal children, partly because of the practical problems a retarded child presents. Such a child, particularly if it is physically handicapped as well, may strain the family's budget by requiring special medical care, individual transportation to medical clinics, and in-home therapy. Baby sitters and day-care facilities will also cost money and may be unavailable to many families. Moreover, such children often require a kind of minute-by-minute supervision not necessary with normal children.

The family as a whole may also suffer from practical problems. For example, it may be difficult to entertain friends at home, visit other friends, attend movies, or go to church together. A study of 200 British families with a severely retarded child in the home listed many problems as being severely disruptive of the family.[2] In the order of their significance, these problems included limitation of family activities, the need for constant supervision, additional financial expense, and physical exhaustion from the need for frequent attention at night. A sample of families of moderately retarded children in Australia felt greatly hindered by their inability to go on family holidays together.[3]

One of the most common features of the relationship between parents and their retarded child is overprotection. Study after study has shown that parents of such children tend to overprotect the child, doing for him what the child could easily be taught to do for himself. This may occur because the mother finds it easier to feed, bathe, or dress the child than to teach the child to do these things independently. In other cases, however, the reason for the overprotection may be psychological, involving the parents' fear that anything that might happen to the child would be the last straw on their own burden of guilt. As we shall see later, there is considerable variation in the ways in which overprotection occurs; in some instances certain ethnic groups may be more protective than others.

The available research is inconclusive regarding the overall impact of a clinically retarded child on its family. As I mentioned before, it appears to be the case that well-integrated, happy families are able to tolerate the birth of such a child, but families in which there is preexisting difficulty may be shattered by the event. In either case, one pattern seems to be clear—next to the mother, the burden of a clinically retarded child in the family tends to fall most heavily on an older normal sister, if there is one in the family. Such a sister frequently takes on the role of caregiver, freeing the mother for other tasks. Where an older normal sister is not available, it is the mother who carries the burden. As we might expect from our knowledge of normal families, fathers and brothers tend to be less involved with the day-to-day care of a clinically retarded child.

Families with clinically retarded children also have long-term problems to which they must adapt. Many families are able to adapt in a positive and effective way. Some, indeed, look upon the child as a blessing and an asset, as did this British family interviewed by Charles Hannam.[4]

CLH   What about the rest of the family?

Mrs. Mercer   Oh, they have been awfully good about it. My eldest boy, he was eleven when Philip was born, and I made my husband tell the children before I came home. I knew very well I was going to be in tears and they would ask why, so I made him tell Richard first, and Richard sat and listened to him and then he said "Can we keep him?" In fact they have been marvelous about him and so have their friends.

CLH   How do they treat him?

Mrs. Mercer   Indulgently. The boy who is twelve now, he got to the model-making stage at the age of six and Philip would sometimes get in the way and then of course there would be a great hoo-ha about it, but they are very fond of him, very tolerant, and very forgiving; they all look after him, too. Everybody has got their eyes and ears open for doors and things like this. The girl who is next to him in age, she is particularly fond of him. They rush into each other's arms when they have been apart for a day.

CLH   Have you sent Philip to the residential unit at the centre?

Mrs. Mercer   No. Never. No. The main objection comes from my children. There is a great cry of "If he were normal you wouldn't dream of doing that." I suggested it when we were going to my niece's twenty-first birthday party; they said they could cope and I said "No, I think I'll put Philip into the residential unit." "Don't you dare," they said, "he doesn't leave until we go to school, we can wait for the bus. We are home before he comes home" . . . We wouldn't dare put him in for a holiday because they adore playing with him on the sands. Each year they would say "I wonder if Philip will go in this time, shall we try this with him, shall we try that with him?" We got him in last year and couldn't get him out.

INSTITUTIONAL CARE

Some families will decide that they must consider placing their retarded child in an institution. Institutional placement is not as common or as popular today as it was in the past, and it has hazards not only for the retarded child but for his siblings, who may feel endangered themselves by the loss of their brother or sister. Nevertheless, physicians continue to advise institutional placement with some frequency, and there are a number of circumstances when a clinically retarded child can best be treated in a large institutional setting.

Large institutions for the mentally retarded date back to the mid-1800s in both the United States and Great Britain. For many years such institutions were the only available placement source for mildly retarded persons. For example, in 1969 a comprehensive survey of residential facilities in the United States showed that 190,000 retarded persons were housed in public institutions and another 65,000 in smaller private institutions of one sort or another. Beginning in the 1960s, recognition grew that these large institutional centers were not too satisfactory. Report after report documented the overcrowding, the isolation, the barrenness, the generally dehumanizing character of these institutions. Mentally retarded persons often lacked privacy, had no social life, were treated in a rigid routine fashion, and had little interaction with the staff or with other patients.

The publicity given to such institutions and their failings led to a general trend toward a shift of patients from large institutions to smaller ones that could provide more individualized and humane treatment surroundings. Though it should not be concluded that all large institutions for the retarded suffered from these many deficiencies or that all continue to suffer from them, it is indeed the case that, in various times and places, institutions showed a high rate of patient mortality soon after admission and that many provided nothing more than custodial care sufficient to keep patients reasonably clean and healthy. Indeed, some institutions have been justly accused of "warehousing" patients in a manner shocking to public morality: naked, feces-soiled patients lying on cold cement floors unattended, unwanted, and often unwell year after year in dirty inhumane circumstances that would do no credit to a zoo.

Frequent studies have attempted to assess the effects of institutional life on clinically retarded children. Generally speaking, when such children are compared with retarded children who are kept at home, the children at home have an advantage in mental development, especially in language, and they exhibit fewer stereotyped, self-stimulating, and self-destructive behaviors. For example, British scientist Jack Tizard removed sixteen severely mentally retarded children from a large and crowded institution and placed them in a small family-type facility. These children subsequently made significantly greater advances in verbal and social development than sixteen matched children who remained behind in the institution.[5] Similar findings have been reported by a number of investigators including D. J. Steadman and D. H. Eichorn, who compared Down's syndrome children living at home with others in a special enrichment unit of a state hospital. These investigators found that, in spite of the stimulation of this special hospital environment, the institutionalized group of children had significantly lower IQ and social development scores than the children who remained at home.[6] Although there can be no doubt that in some instances the parental home is a very poor environment, and the child is better placed in an institution, there is little evidence to show that institutional placement generally confers any advantage over the home environment, except, of course, when the child requires medical care not available in a family setting. This is particularly true when such children are placed early in life; young children suffer much greater handicaps in mental and social development when placed in an institution than do children who are institutionalized later in life, especially in adolescence or as adults.

In considering the issue of institutionalizing a clinically retarded child, it would be a mistake to concentrate solely upon the consequences for the child, since consequences for the parents can be quite serious. Frequently, clinically retarded children are institutionalized because of severe behavior disorders at home which have disrupted the family, upset the siblings, and made life virtually impossible for everyone. Once the child has left home, however, even though the disruptive behavior leaves with him, parents may begin to idealize the child and feel that their decision was a poor one. Such parents may feel guilt regarding their decision or, in an effort to defend themselves psychologically against the guilt of "putting him away," they may literally abandon the child and pay no further attention to him. Sometimes the removal of a retarded child from the family may actually increase the problems that a family faces. The child sometimes serves as a scapegoat and, when the scapegoat is removed, other more disruptive problems come to the fore. Still, though, there is no sound empirical evidence to show when institutional placement will lead to an improvement or to a deterioration in family functioning.

There are many poignant and powerful accounts of parents faced with the decision of institutionalization. The ordeal of Pearl Buck in searching for an institutional home for her daughter is a touching example.[7] It is important to keep in mind the fact that for many families institutionalization is not only the best decision they can make for their child—it is the only one possible. Yet the choice is a traumatic one and it is often difficult to find a suitable institution. The American writer Josh Greenfeld has written two moving books about the problems in finding a home for his retarded son Noah, and his article on this for *Life* magazine received the largest mail response by readers of any piece in the long history of that magazine.[8]

COMMUNITY ADJUSTMENT

There is some evidence to suggest that adults who as children had IQs under 50 can in certain circumstances become well integrated into community life. A 1956 survey of over one thousand individuals who had IQs below 50 as children in Birmingham, England, discovered that 14 percent of the women and 26 percent of the men were employed, and only 4 percent were living in institutions. Although it should be noted that there was plentiful employment in Birmingham at that point in history, this is nevertheless an impressive finding.

A more detailed study in the United States gives us an even clearer perspective on the potential of clinically retarded people for life in community settings. In 1957, Gerhart Saenger followed up the lives of 520 retarded adults whose IQs were between 40 and 50 (that is, in the moderately retarded range of clinical retardation) who had been former students in special classes for the mentally retarded in New York City.[9] Saenger found that 8 percent of these individuals were dead, 26 percent had been placed in large state institutions, but the remainder—two thirds of the sample—were living with their families in the community. As might be expected, wide variations were found in family conditions and attitudes, but in general these moderately retarded persons were accepted in family life. Most of their parents were judged to be emotionally well-adjusted, with slightly better adjustments among parents of retarded people who were living at home. Only a few parents, one in nine, considered the retarded person to be a major problem for themselves or the siblings. In half the cases, sincere concern and affection were expressed for the retarded person by all members of the family. More remarkably, three out of ten parents appeared to encourage independent behavior. Overprotection was found more frequently when a physical handicap existed. Overprotection was also more common among the parents of Jewish background.

Those people who were in an institution appear to have been so placed because of behavior problems: restlessness, hyperactivity, temper tantrums, tendencies to harm themselves, running away, destructiveness, violence, sexual delinquency. Of the retarded persons living at home one half were able to interact with their families in a relatively normal, even though limited, manner. Ten percent were unable to interact in any satisfactory sense, and the balance showed intermediate degrees of successful adaptation to family life. Much of the success of the adaptation appeared to relate to total family atmosphere. Almost all these retarded persons spent most of their time in solitary activities, with very little time spent in constructive leisure-time activities. Not much time was spent outside of the home, but the great majority did assume some responsibilities around the house. Very few required special attention.

The social life of these moderately retarded adults living in the community was characterized by loneliness and solitude, even though their families accepted them and even though they had some degree of mobility and self-reliance. Thus, 78 percent went out of the home by themselves at least occasionally, but few ventured out of their own neighborhood. Most spent their time "hanging around" in a solitary fashion and literally doing nothing. Few had friendships and those that did exist were of a limited nature. Twenty-five percent had friends of the opposite sex, but in most instances these contacts seemed to be social only. Twenty percent professed interest in marriage, but none was reported to have been married.

Saenger reported that community acceptance of these retarded individuals varied with the socioeconomic makeup of the neighborhood. Hostility was commonly found in neighborhoods of low income, low education, and high social mobility. The hostility was not related to physical handicap or level of functioning, but it did reflect in various ways the popularity of the parents and the behavior of the retarded persons. In spite of this hostility, only 11 percent of the retarded adults had got into any kind of trouble with the law.

Perhaps the most remarkable finding of Saenger's study is that 27 percent of the sample residing in the community were employed on a full- or part-time basis. Of these, fully 85 percent worked in competitive employment, most of them in the neighborhood in which they lived. The jobs most frequently concerned the delivery of parcels from local stores, for tips rather than a salary, and various kinds of cleaning and janitorial work.

Saenger's study indicates that adults with a moderate level of retardation have the ability to adjust to adult life in a community setting. However, in contrast to the more mildly retarded people we shall discuss later, these clinically retarded persons do not "disappear into the general population" when they become adults. They continue to be seen as mentally retarded, and they continue to be largely dependent upon social agencies or other people. There is little to suggest that they can be socially independent, but there is much to indicate that, with the support of their families, they can live relatively normal lives in community settings.

More recent research in the United States and England confirms Saenger's findings, suggesting that such people can not only adapt well to life in their own families, but in some circumstances can do so in community residential facilities. For example, the work of Arnold Birenbaum and Samuel Seiffer reports the experiences of some 48 former residents of three large state institutions who were transferred to a small community facility in a large metropolitan area (eastern United States).[10] These people, who lived in what was similar to a large boardinghouse, had an average IQ of 51 and an average age of thirty-three. The facility was coeducational. The residents, many of whom were clinically retarded, generally found this setting to be a positive change from the large institutions. In the community setting they had two-person rooms, made their own meals, and left the facility each day to work in a sheltered workshop; all were free to travel about the city on public transportation, and many established relationships with members of the opposite sex, usually through their workshop experiences. The following quotation gives a sense of the experience of living in this setting:

A man in his early thirties lives in a large city. It's seven A.M., the alarm rings in his room. His roommate has long since gone to work and after turning off the alarm, he gets up, washes, shaves, brushes his teeth and has his breakfast. He gets his sandwich for lunch and meets a fellow worker with whom he travels by bus to the shop. At the end of the work day they return home together. Later, with his dinner companions, he discusses the events of the day and his plans for the weekend. After dinner he watches television, has a snack and talks to a friend about the program on the screen. After saying good night, he goes off to his room where he finds his roommate already asleep. Tomorrow, he thinks, he will have to clean up their room. He turns on the radio very softly, so as not to disturb his roommate, in order to relax before going to sleep. He sets his alarm clock so that he will wake up at seven o'clock and be able to arrive at work by the required time. Tomorrow is pay day and he thinks about what he will do with the money. Perhaps he will go to the new James Bond movie at the local theater.[11]

The man being described here has an IQ of 51 and spent eighteen years in a large institution before moving to the community setting. The initial reaction of these moderately retarded people to their new residence was highly favorable. After a year and a half, some of them felt less enthusiastic about their new home, but these feelings appeared to be related primarily to a higher level of aspiration; that is, some of these people had become restive in their new environment because they now wanted to be completely independent and completely "normal." On the whole, however, residents continued to view the community setting as a positive and beneficial one. Their parents looked upon the experiment somewhat differently. Their initial reaction was extremely guarded and sometimes downright frightened. They were concerned that their children would be unable to work on their own, to travel in the city, or to cope with the vices of a city environment. After a year and a half, in which their adult children had proven themselves capable of coping with city life, parental attitudes became dramatically more positive.

The principal area in which these clinically retarded people had difficulty with the new environment had to do with the demands for appropriate public behavior; since they had no specific training in how to live and work in a large city, they needed to know how to behave at crosswalks, how to ride the subway, not to stare at others in public, how to dress and groom themselves, how to avoid unwanted eye contact on a public street, and how to avoid dangerous areas at night. Many did poorly. In all cases, however, these failings were ones that could have been corrected by a specific training program. Many of these retarded people learned to be quite competent in public places after they had some experience with them.

Another significant project, this time concerning clinically retarded children rather than adults, has been taking place over the last decade in the Wessex region of southern England. A special epidemiological survey of mental handicap was undertaken, and a register of all mentally handicapped persons has been maintained since 1963. It was learned that 80 percent of all severely retarded children in Wessex live at home, and 20 percent were in institutions. However, 40 percent of all severely mentally handicapped adults were at home, and 60 percent were in institutions, indicating that as the severely retarded became older, institutional care more frequently became the choice of their families. In the Wessex region, an area with a population of close to three million, a number of what are called "locally based hospital units" have been established to complement the existing larger hospital institutions. These locally based units are small, with a maximum of twenty-five beds, and are situated in residential streets and urban centers serving populations that range from rural to urban. Their location is determined by their access to public transportation, shopping facilities, recreational areas, and other places that are part of normal daily living. These units are furnished as far as possible to resemble homes, and they come with fully equipped kitchens, laundries, and attractively designed furniture.

These units have been in operation for approximately ten years, and a very large amount of systematic research has been conducted under the direction of Albert Kushlick. Kushlick and his colleagues find that the severely retarded children in the locally based hospital units have attained higher levels of social activity during the day than have similar children who reside in traditional large hospital units in the Wessex region. Similarly, children in the locally based units have achieved levels of adaptive behavior equal to or better than those of clinically retarded children in the large hospitals, and they have established higher rates of contact with parents and other people outside the facility. At the same time, the mortality rate of these severely handicapped children is the same as that of children in the larger hospitals. Parents and relatives of these children, compared with parents and relatives of children in traditional hospitals, have visited their children more often, discussed the problems their children suffer with professionals more often, and are more satisfied with the services their children receive.

These very positive findings are in direct opposition to one belief that has been widely discussed by various British writers—that it is not feasible to maintain at reasonable cost severely handicapped, mentally retarded people in small residential units. Kushlick and his colleagues find that it is indeed possible to do so, both with children and adults, and the cost of doing so is no greater, and in many instances less, than what would be required to maintain such clinically retarded children in large hospitals.[12]

Despite the success of these small residential facilities, it is clear that the majority of severely handicapped children remain in their parental homes. In an effort to improve conditions in these homes, Kushlick and his colleagues have developed a plan for teaching parents the skills required to implement training in their own home. The plan used by the Wessex group is similar to one developed in Portage, Wisconsin. This plan involves a three- to seven-day training period by which people with no previous experience or training go out into homes, and using the methods of behavior analysis developed by R. G. Tharp and R. J. Wetzell, teach parents how to set and achieve educational goals for their own children.[13] In both the United States and Great Britain, this program has proven to be a highly efficient way of delivering and maintaining a service with a relatively small amount of time by specialists.[14]

A final issue involves the inevitable aging of the severely

retarded. As we have seen in the work of Hannam and others, one of the greatest fears that parents face is that their severely retarded child will grow old and there will be no one to care for him. This is a legitimate concern, to be sure, but the previously mentioned research of Saenger, and Birenbaum and Seiffer, as well as the development of locally based hospital units in Great Britain, makes it clear that we are moving toward the development of resources that will permit the successful adaptation of older clinically retarded persons to life outside the large institutions which had been their only alternative once their parents died or became too old to care for them.

5/ Sociocultural Retardation

Clinical retardation is a heartrending problem for all too many people. It is sobering to realize, then, that clinical retardation constitutes no more than 25 percent of all mental retardation; the remainder of retarded people fall into the category of what is commonly known as sociocultural retardation. These people were once referred to as "morons" or "feebleminded." Later they were termed "familial" or "cultural-familial" to emphasize the fact that the disorder seemed to "run in families" and had something to do with cultural disadvantage. Most recently, they have been identified as persons with "mental retardation associated with psychosocial disadvantage." Whatever the term—and I shall use "sociocultural retardation" here for reasons that will soon become clear—the degree of intellectual impairment is mild, with IQ between 55 and 69. Usually there are no easily demonstrable signs of physical disability. For reasons that are still not determined, 65 percent of the sociocultural retarded are male; some experts relate this disproportion to a presumed biological advantage of females, who are in many ways more robust than males, but others point to the higher expectations that society has for males.

Perhaps most significantly, socioculturally retarded children often come from those social groups that are economically, educationally, and socially disadvantaged. I have already mentioned that a child born and raised in an urban ghetto or an impoverished rural environment is fifteen times more likely to be labeled mentally retarded than a child of the same age from suburbia. Various investigators have found a similar disadvantage for lower-class children in Great Britain.[1] For example, in a careful study of Aberdeen, Scotland, Herbert Birch and his colleagues found that sociocultural retardation was nine times more common among the lower classes than it was among the upper classes.[2] Sociocultural retardation was associated with low income, crowding, poor housing, and large families in which the mothers held unskilled jobs prior to marriage.

Before we look at the specific conditions and circumstances linked to sociocultural retardation, let me illustrate the social and cultural context of the phenomenon by examining a community in the Appalachian Mountains of eastern Kentucky.

AN APPALACHIAN HOLLOW

As described by Rena Gazaway in 1969,[3] the 238 inhabitants of Duddie's Branch, a hollow (neighborhood) in Appalachia, are a startling example of a community of people in the contemporary United States so isolated, impoverished, and ignorant of the world around them that the entire population can be considered mentally retarded. The inhabitants of Duddie's Branch live in ramshackle wood and tarpaper shacks along a one-mile stretch of a badly polluted stream. Since the present-day Duddie's Branchers, like their ancestors, are illiterate, there are no records to tell us where these people came from or how long they have lived in this remote mountain region. We do know that these white so-called hillbillies are primarily of English, Scots, and Irish descent, and that they have lived in this area for several generations.

A few of the Duddie's Branchers are employed, mostly in coalmines, and some farm a little, but most of them survive on government welfare payments. All are grindingly poor, with family incomes averaging less than $2000 per year. Not surprisingly, they are very badly nourished, typically depending on a high sugar diet and whatever food the welfare program dispenses. Not only is there little protein available, there is little food of any kind, and most Duddie's Branchers are hungry. The children, particularly, are chronically malnourished; they are very thin and small. Some six-year-olds have achieved less than half the growth that is normal for children their age, and many of them are anemic.

For many reasons, disease is endemic. For one thing, there is terrible overcrowding, with several adults and children piled into the same bed at night. They also live in filth. The people rarely wash themselves, and then only their hands and face; their interest in hygiene does not include cleaning their shacks or washing their pots and dishes. As a result, cockroaches are everywhere. Also their water supply is polluted, in part because most Duddie's Branchers merely defecate on the ground outside their shacks, leaving their feces for the chickens to eat, and in part because almost everything is dumped into the stream. Their ill health is also related to the fact that their shacks leak and are poorly heated in the winter. Many adults are chronically ill, especially with tuberculosis, and the children are always covered with sores and their noses run all the time. As Gazaway puts it, "the housekeeping is shocking and the filth defies description. The air is foul with the stifling odor of dried urine, stale cooking, unwashed bodies, dirty clothing . . . A wide variety of bugs and rodents, which claim squatter's rights to every corner and loose board, leisurely emerge from their territories and trek to the generous hunting ground—the floor."[4]

Keep in mind that Gazaway was fond of these people and understanding of the circumstances in which they lived. Yet some of their customs would horrify even the most sympathetic outsiders. They sometimes shoot pets such as dogs just because it pleases them to do so, and adult men rather commonly have intercourse with girls as young as six. When illegitimate children result from unions with unmarried girls, no one is particularly concerned. Gazaway reports this reaction from one boy: " 'Hain't 'xactly sure 'bout my paw, but reckon I's got one some whar." Nor is he curious about his parent. " 'Hain't worth knowin'."[5] If marriage is indifferently conceived, so is community; the Duddie's Branchers have no community groups or formal organizations. Indeed, no family belongs to any group, not even a church. Church activities do not exist and formal religion is thought to be irrelevant.

Duddie's Branch is both isolated from the outside world and ignorant of its ways. It is perhaps not surprising that Duddie's Branchers never brush their teeth (Napoleon never bathed or brushed his teeth either), but it must be considered remarkable that people living in contemporary American society have no knowledge of eating utensils; they eat with their fingers. All but a few Duddie's Branchers are illiterate, and so despite the presence of some television sets in the hollow, these people have almost no knowledge of the world around them. Only a handful have traveled farther than a few miles outside the hollow, and the most knowledgeable man in Duddie's Branch did not know the capital of the United States or the name of any president. However, he had heard of the "American King"—his name was Kennedy.

In addition to malnutrition, disease, and isolation, Duddie's Branch is a community of astonishing intellectual impoverishment. Its adult inhabitants not only cannot read, they have no conception of either clock time or calendrical time. So they are capable of only the most general temporal calculations based on day and night or changes in the seasons. Most adults cannot even make change for money and are often victimized by nearby storekeepers as a result. In response to Gazaway's inquiries about being cheated by merchants, one man said:

> "Things costs diff'r'nt. Sometimes I comes in hyur with a couple 'a skins (two dollars) 'n' leaves out with lard, flour, 'baccer (tobacco) 'n' candy on a stick fur th' younguns, 'n' th' next time I only gits one can 'a 'baccer 'n' caint git th' younguns nothin'."
>
> "What do you suppose is the reason for that?" I prodded.
>
> "Don't reckon I kin figger 'ese fellers."[6]

Some of the adults in Duddie's Branch are ashamed to acknowledge their illiteracy and are embarrassed when, by virtue of making an X, they admit that they cannot write their names. Gazaway says that when they are requested to sign a document, they will ask, "Will a cross do?" The diagonal lines of an X are a cross to them. " 'Haint no point takin' time t' write m' name w'en a cross'll do,' they sheepishly add."[7]

Duddie's Branchers speak a dialect of English that outsiders in nearby Kentucky towns can barely understand, but in addition to this communicative limitation, they have a very limited vocabulary even among themselves, and in fact they seldom use the vocabulary they do have. Thus, despite her excellent rapport with these people, for some time Gazaway actually thought that most adults were mute. She reports that during the course of an ordinary day and evening, a family may not exchange half a dozen words. Adults not only have few words for each other, but they seldom communicate with their children and then only in the most laconic fashion.

The men of Duddie's Branch possess few employable skills; only four of them could be considered even semiskilled. Women seldom work, perhaps because they are almost perpetually pregnant, a state of affairs that led to a problem for one family which can be used to illustrate the intellectual capacities of adults in Duddie's Branch. One woman, Dana, experienced a difficult birth with her ninth child; surprisingly she was then taken to a doctor, who told her not to become pregnant again. After much resistance, her husband (a man perhaps appropriately named Letcher) agreed, but would permit only one form of birth control—the oral pill. Gazaway recounts the consequences as follows:

> I gave Dana a big wall calendar and a pencil and told her to cross out the date each day that she took a pill. We practiced by marking the previous month and she seemed to understand what she was to do. Because she was unable to rotate the dispenser, which enabled one tablet at a time to drop out, we put all of the pills into a big, open-mouthed bottle. Four days later I checked on her. She said that she had taken a pill every day but could not mark the calendar because the children had taken the pencil. Twenty-eight of the thirty pills were still in the bottle, even though she professed to have taken four. I gave her another pencil which we tied to a string and hung around her neck. Two or three days after that she told me that she needed another "writin." I thought that she meant another pencil, but she was talking about a calendar. She had crossed off the entire month and still had most of the pills.
>
> "Why did you cross off the whole page Dana?" I was baffled. "I 'uz scaret th' pencil might be losted agin 'n' I marked th' time paper afore th' younguns got aholt 'a hit," she confessed.[8]

Undaunted, Gazaway gave her another calendar and at the end of the week returned to see how she was progressing. Not a single date had been crossed off. Had she lost the pencil again? No, she said. Then why hadn't this been marked? She hadn't made marks because she hadn't taken the pills. Why not? She said that her husband Letcher had a backache and he took them. Gazaway explained to Letcher that the pills were not for backache, but he said they were the only medication that had ever helped him. The next day, Gazaway took more pills to Dana. She was confident that everything would finally be alright. Dana knew how to cross off the squares on the calendar, her pencil was protected, and Letcher's backache was no longer troubling him. However, when Gazaway next saw her she was told that Dana now had trouble remembering whether or not she had taken a pill. The count could not be an accurate record of how many days Dana had missed because on some days she had inexplicably taken more than one pill. Several months later Dana became pregnant again. She announced that the pills were the cause of her pregnancy. Letcher remained convinced that the pills were a cure for his backaches. Gazaway was frustrated, to say the least.

In this isolated, culturally and linguistically deprived environment, children before the age of six interact primarily with one another. According to Gazaway, they speak and walk later than children do in the "outside world"; they also have less curiosity and imagination, and they learn more slowly. Parents do nothing to educate or stimulate their children, and most parents oppose schooling altogether. Since school attendance for the children of Duddie's Branch is not enforced by Kentucky authorities, most children go to school only sporadically if at all, and those who do attend drop out early in life. By school standards and by psychometric evaluation, these children are mentally retarded. Gazaway provides this remarkable illustration:

> Hollow parents are completely indifferent to the expanding demands for more formal and informal educational experiences. Not one child from Duddie's Branch has ever seen a sandbox. None has played with finger paints, puzzles, or blocks. Their "toys" consist of broken bottles, sharp metal, discarded tin cans. Ask them about Goldilocks, and they will look at you in bewilderment—they have never heard a fairy tale. I made a bean bag from an old rag and asked some of the older boys to catch it. They had difficulty. With an old string ball and a heavy stick, I tried to involve them in batting practice. I was unsuccessful. Not

only do games fail to interest them, they are almost completely unable to participate in most activities. They could not be taught to whistle, sing, or even hum a simple tune. I wrote 1111 2222 3--- --4- -55- on a sheet of paper and asked a number of eight-year-olds who had never been to school to fill in the missing numbers. They could not. Nor were they able to draw a circle, a square, raise their right arms, raise their left arms, extend their fingers, or spell their names. I showed them a series of pictures pasted on cardboard; cat, dog, raccoon, rabbit, otter, rat, squirrel.
"What are they?" I inquired.
"Reckon they's cats," they decided.[9]

The incompetence of Duddie's Branch children is by no means confined to "intellectual" skills. The following example illustrates the kind of incompetence these children display in many areas of life that are presumably familiar to them:

One boy said that he wanted to be a carpenter.
"Can you drive a nail, Zeb?"
"If'n hit hain't restin' in green (going through green lumber)."
"Can you use a ruler?"
"Yep."
"How much does a ruler measure?"
"Right smart."
"Is a ruler and a yard stick the same length?"
"Reckon."
"How much is a foot?"
He looked at me quizically and then pointed to his foot.
"Reckon a foot's a foot."
"Show me how much a yard is."
"Twit me 'n' 'at tree."
The distance he indicated was at least four yards.
"That's a long yard."
"Measurin' hain't long 'r short."[10]

These children could not saw a two-inch straight line—indeed, they had great difficulty in using a saw at all. They had no concept of a cutting edge or where the sawing would take place. They were no better at hammering nails. Gazaway gave each boy ten nails of different lengths (each boy had identical different lengths). She timed each one to see how long it took him to drive the ten nails into a soft redwood board. Gazaway herself pounded in ten identical nails in fifteen seconds. The closest any one of the boys came to that time was twenty minutes, and even then all of the nailheads were not flush with the surface of the board.

In this community so marked by disease, malnutrition, overcrowding, neglect, limited language use, and cultural deprivation, children grow up who are mentally retarded by the standards of nearby schools and communities. Their illiterate, uninformed parents, too, would almost certainly be considered mentally retarded in the outside world. Few if any could be expected to score as much as 70 on an IQ test, and their adaptive behavior outside Duddie's Branch is appallingly poor, as witness their lack of job skills, illiteracy, and inability to make change or tell time. Here, then, is an entire community of people who are incompetent to live outside their isolated mountain neighborhood. They make no attempt to move away into this larger world and remain in their hollow where they survive, if marginally, with the assistance of public welfare and food supplements.

It is not surprising that they reject the outside world, but they also express fierce loyalty to their own way of life. So successful are they in their rejection of the larger culture that their children remain in Duddie's Branch and are happy to do so. Are these people competent, then, within their own community? That is difficult to determine, since while Gazaway lists the many ways in which they are ignorant, she also reports that they can be "crafty," especially in manipulating the welfare system, and she indicates many ways in which they exhibit what appears to be adaptive intelligence and insight in their everyday lives. And to be sure, they often express love and compassion for one another and for outsiders like Gazaway whom they accept. Is their incompetence solely a product of their long cultural isolation and their illiteracy, or is it also a function of in-breeding, malnutrition, disease, obstetrical injuries, and other biological factors that may have produced lasting intellectual deficits? The answer, unfortunately, is that we don't know. Gazaway attempted a natural experiment concerning the learning ability of these children by taking one of the brightest of these boys to the "outside world" with her. After initial difficulty, he seemed to be making progress but he soon became homesick and returned to the hollow.

The Duddie's Branchers, then, more than exemplify the phenomenon of sociocultural retardation. Like other socioculturally retarded people, they score below 70 on IQ tests and do very poorly in school. Like the Duddie's Branchers, the great majority of socioculturally retarded persons come from areas of great poverty where there is widespread disease and malnutrition, and little encouragement to succeed in school or to adopt the behaviors and values of the mainstream culture. There are three general issues to be considered about sociocultural retardation. First, why does it occur? Second, what happens to such people? And, finally, what implication does the existence of these people have for society?

6 / The Environment

The central fact about sociocultural retardation is that it occurs most of the time among social groups that are poor, uneducated, and culturally different. That much we know. But what exactly causes it? Is it cultural deprivation in which children are not stimulated to learn? Is it a product of disease or malnutrition? Is it something about the physical environment? Or since it is in school that their intellectual deficiencies are most often first recognized, is it something about the school system itself that produces sociocultural retardation?

ENRICHING THE CULTURAL ENVIRONMENT

Since sociocultural retardation occurs primarily among the poor and culturally isolated, and since there is rarely any known physical basis for this retardation, many programs have been developed in an attempt to enrich the cultural environment of such people. Project Head Start, begun in 1965, is a famous example of this sort of effort. The rationale for such programs is the widespread belief that early experience plays a major causal role in determining the intelligence of a child. Earlier in this century, many psychologists such as Galton, Cattell, and Hall believed that intelligence was largely inherited and therefore could not be changed significantly by experience. The development of the IQ test was founded on this belief. A contrary view was expressed—and greatly overstated—by the famous environmentalist, J. B. Watson:

> Give me a dozen healthy infants, well-formed, and my own specified world to bring them up in and I'll guarantee to take any

59

one at random and train him to become any type of specialist I might select—a doctor, lawyer, artist, merchant-chief and, yes, even beggar and thief, regardless of the talents, penchants, tendencies, abilities, vocations, and race of his ancestors.[1]

Although the IQ test became established, with the idea that IQ was fixed relatively early in life, environmentalists nevertheless held to the belief that early experience could influence the development of intelligence. While no responsible scientist in recent years has accepted fully the utopian views of Watson, some have insisted overmuch on the power of environmental change to eliminate sociocultural retardation, as psychologist Edward Zigler indicates in this trenchant comment:

In the educational realm, this has spelled itself out in the use of panaceas, gadgets and gimmicks of the most questionable sort. It is the environmentalist who suggests to parents how easy it is to raise the child's IQ and who has prematurely led many to believe that the retarded could be made normal, and the normal made geniuses.[2]

Nevertheless, general scientific opinion has favored the idea that IQ does change to some degree during the course of a person's life and that these changes are presumably in response to education or other environmental factors.[3] This opinion is based in part on experiments with animals, particularly apes, and partly on research that showed improvement in IQ when children were moved from an "unstimulating" environment such as an orphanage to a more normal one. Many such studies have been conducted with retarded children and adults, and most appear to show that IQs do rise if the cultural environment is improved, especially if the improvement is made in early childhood.

However, early environmental enrichment programs have not always succeeded in raising the IQ of participating children, and even when IQs have been increased, they frequently fall to the original starting point when the program is terminated. Many of the Head Start programs followed this pattern. Some critics such as A. R. Jensen call this phenomenon a "hot house" effect in which the IQ can be artificially raised somewhat only to drop again when treatment ends. Other critics admit that exceptionally deprived or isolated environments can restrict the development of intelligence, but they point out that most children who live in city slums or rural isolation do *not* become mentally retarded, suggesting that something more than a deprived cultural environment must be at work. In recent years, skepticism about the effects of early experience on intelligence has grown, but instead of concluding that environment has no effect on intelligence, these critics believe that early experience does not fix intelligence once and for all; instead, they say, later experience can overcome the effects even of an extremely deprived early environment.[4]

An illustration of evidence for the idea that intelligence is not necessarily set by early experience comes from psychologist Jerome Kagan, who did research in an isolated part of Guatemala. In the small, remote farming village that Kagan studied, infants typically spend their first year of life isolated in a tiny darkened hut. Not only are these Indian children not played with, they are not even spoken to. In addition to this almost complete neglect, the infants are badly nourished, and they experience continuing gastrointestinal and respiratory illness. When Kagan compared these children with American babies of the same age, the Guatemalan children were mentally retarded. In the development of mental abilities and language, these children were between two and twelve months behind their American counterparts. For example, while American children begin to speak their first words at about eighteen months, the Guatemalan children do not begin to speak until sometime between the thirtieth and thirty-sixth months of life.

By the second year of life, conditions change for the Guatemalan children. They are permitted to move about outside their huts, and they begin to develop an interest in people, animals, and objects. By the age of four or five, they play with other children, and by eight or nine they begin to take on some responsibilities on the family farm, and they do some domestic chores around the hut. However, until the age of ten, these children are intellectually far inferior to children of the same age in the United States. Moreover, their performance on various tests of perception, memory, and reasoning is also inferior to that of other Indian children from a nearby village who are not so completely isolated during their first year of life. Nevertheless, by the time these "retarded" children reach adolescence, they perform almost as well as American children do on intellectual tests. Kagan concludes that any differences in performance that remain between the Guatemalan and American children are likely to be due to the fact that the Guatemalan children continue to experience relatively poor schooling and cultural deprivation, rather than the isolation and lack of stimulation they experienced as infants.[5]

The best known and most extensive research on early environmental enrichment is the Milwaukee Project, directed by Rick Heber.[6] Heber and his colleagues first selected an area in Milwaukee that had the lowest average family income, the most deteriorated housing, and the densest population in the city. Although only 5 percent of the city's population lived in this area, about 33 percent of the socioculturally retarded children in Milwaukee's schools came from this small part of the city. The researchers then selected mothers in this area who had already had another child aged six, and from these mothers they sampled eighty-eight consecutive births. When IQ tests were given, there was a strong similarity between the IQs of the mothers and their children. The researchers then selected fifty mothers with IQs below 75; mothers with IQs over 100 were chosen as a comparison group.

As soon as the newborn infant came home from the hospital with its "retarded" mother, a member of Heber's staff began working with both mother and infant in an effort to stimulate language learning, problem solving, and motivation to learn and achieve. Various educational programs continued to take place over the first sixty months of life for the "retarded" sample at an estimated cost of $30,000 per child. The children of mothers with IQs over 100 received no environmental enrichment. At age sixty months, the children of the retarded mothers had an average IQ 26 points higher than that of the children with normal-IQ mothers. At age nine, after three years of public school, the "retarded" children had an average IQ of 106 while the normal controls who received no intervention had an average IQ of only 79. Subsequently, however, there has been some loss of IQ for the retarded children, apparently because of a loss of motivation on the part of the mothers to continue the program. It remains to be seen, then, whether the elaborate enrichment of the Milwaukee Project produced lasting gains in IQ or whether it simply created a hot-house effect.

As almost everyone involved in efforts to enrich the environment of retarded children is aware, such efforts are costly, time-consuming, and tremendously complex. It is this complexity that makes efforts to improve an environment so difficult. What does one wish to improve? The list of theoretically relevant variables is a long one. There is a host of factors involving the child's prenatal environment: the mother's health and nutrition, the spacing of births, obstetrical care, and even family size. For example, it has been shown that first-borns have higher IQs than later births. This phenomenon may have biological causes (a better intrauterine environment or more conscientious medical care, say), or it may simply be that a first-born or only child gets more attention from parents.[7]

But variables of this sort are only part of the picture. Also relevant is the role of parental aspirations for their children's education. Do parents want their children to do well? Do they tutor them in preschool years and watch over their homework after they enter school? Or do they leave their children to themselves or to the caregiving of other children? Are the language models used in the home congruent with "school language," or must the child learn a new vocabulary, accent, and grammar in order to do well in school? Does the general quality of life in the home encourage intellectual growth by the use of games, toys, or hobbies, or is the home crowded, chaotic, and unpredictable? Do mothers talk to their children, use abstract words, and teach them to think for themselves, or do they simply issue orders and try to control the children so that they make as little fuss as possible? Research indicates that many middle-class mothers tend to do the former, while lower-class mothers do the latter.[8]

The list of potentially significant features of a child's environment could go on almost endlessly. Even then we might have missed the most significant factor. The point is that we simply do not yet know what features of a child's environment are most important if the child is to develop normal intelligence. We know that heredity is important, as are many biological considerations. So, we know, is school. Let us continue our exploration of factors related to sociocultural retardation by considering the physical environment itself.

THE PHYSICAL ENVIRONMENT: LEAD

Slogans demanding that the environment be saved or reclaimed are not merely vacuous expressions of human frustration brought about by population growth and man's apparently unlimited capacity to foul his own nest. Where mental retardation is at issue, there can be little doubt that man *has* created a dangerous environment. The list of potential hazards is long—mercury poisoning, radiation, pesticides, nitrates, and perhaps most alarming of all, lead poisoning.

Considering the many uses to which man has long put lead, it is not at all remarkable that lead is now probably the most widespread and dangerous poison affecting man. As a gasoline additive, an ingredient in paint and insecticides, or a component of batteries, vinyl plastic, rubber, and the like, lead is an inescapable feature of the modern world—it is in our air, water, dirt, dust, and food. Like it or not, because we eat and breathe, lead is in us, and while the World Health Organization has set standards for the tolerable limits of lead intake for adults, what is safe for children has not yet been determined.

Lead is a poison that interferes with cellular metabolism. There is no benefit to be had from its presence in the body; it circulates throughout the body in the blood, and when present in large concentrations it is stored in the bones. It produces irritability, loss of appetite, nausea, constipation, and various other gastrointestinal symptoms. Its effects on the blood include both a reduction in hemoglobin production and the destruction of red blood cells, leading to anemia. Its effects on the nervous system range from mild neurological problems and hyperactivity to severe mental retardation. In large amounts it can cause irreversible brain damage, even death.

Because developing tissues are particularly susceptible to lead poisoning, and because children absorb more lead than adults do, they are the most common and most severely affected victims. It has been estimated that each year at least 200 children in the United States die of classical lead poisoning. Another 12,000 to 16,000 are treated and survive, but about half of these survive only to be mentally retarded.[9] However, since only a small percentage of the children who are affected ever receive treatment, it is impossible to estimate how many children may actually become mentally retarded as a result of lead poisoning.

What is even more alarming is the fact that levels of blood lead that were thought to be safe even fifteen years ago are now suspected of being very dangerous indeed. Thus for many years, children whose blood levels were in the 30 to 50 micrograms per 100 ml of whole-blood range were largely ignored. These children did not have classical lead poisoning and their symptoms, if any, went unrecorded. Recent screening in the United States has disclosed that many children from Maine to California have elevated blood-lead levels in this range. For example, a study in Los Angeles found that many black and Chicano children in a low-income area, bounded by two freeways and containing major industry, had elevated blood-lead levels. These children not only live in poor housing painted with lead-based paint, they are continually exposed to automotive exhaust. Depending upon the kind of measurement employed, between 14 percent and 23 percent of the 1239 children tested had blood levels of 30 micrograms per 100 ml or greater. Children in northern California areas not so severely exposed to exhaust or lead-based paint were less severely affected, with only 2 to 6 percent having blood-lead levels in this same range.[10]

What are the consequences of blood-lead levels of this magnitude? The simple answer is that no one knows. For example, no testing of IQ or academic achievement was done with the children in Los Angeles. In another study, this time in Birmingham, England, it was reported that children who lived close to a lead-polluting industrial complex did as well in school as other Birmingham children who lived in an area free of lead dust.[11] Unfortunately, this study did not test for social-class differences among the children or for differences in education offered by the schools involved. More significantly, it did not actually measure the blood-lead levels of the children, so we cannot know how seriously various children were affected by the prevalent lead dust. Another British report issued in 1978 found that as many as five million Britons are regularly drinking water that contains dangerous amounts of lead. These persons live in 1.5 million homes containing old lead pipes that produce cumulative poisoning. A similar danger exists in many older cities in the United States.

We must keep in mind that while we are all exposed to lead in various ways, the poor, especially children of the poor, are most likely to be exposed to large amounts of lead. Old houses are far more likely to have been painted with lead-based paint, and that old paint is likely to be chipping away so that hungry or curious children can eat it. As I mentioned earlier, children suffering from pica may compulsively eat such paint chips, and only a few chips a day for two or three months can be enough to cause fatal lead poisoning in small children. It is also older, deteriorating housing that is likely to have lead water pipes. Industrial sources of lead most often affect low-income people who live nearby, not people in more distant suburbs. And automotive exhaust is likely to be most damaging in heavily traveled inner-city areas.

But poor and culturally isolated populations may also suffer from serious poisoning even when they live in rural areas far from city sources of lead. For example, it has long been reported that North American Indian children on reservations often sniff gasoline in order to get high. Tetraethyl lead inhaled by sniffing leaded gasoline is even more toxic than lead absorbed from most urban sources. A recent systematic study of gasoline sniffing among children on a Canadian Indian reservation indicated that up to half of the children in this community suffered from tetraethyl lead poisoning. The authors conclude that gasoline sniffing and consequent lead poisoning may constitute a "major medical and social problem" not only for Indian populations but in many isolated communities throughout North America.[12]

Another recent study suggests that children with blood-lead levels even lower than 30 micrograms per 100 ml may be at significant risk for mild mental retardation. Oliver David and his associates studied mentally retarded patients in an institution in New York, comparing those with known or suspected etiology with patients for whom there was no known etiology and with normal, nonretarded children.[13] The investigators found that the retarded children with no known etiology—and this is almost always the case in sociocultural retardation—had statistically significantly higher blood-lead levels than either the retarded patients with known etiology or the normal children. Yet the levels recorded for these high blood-lead children only averaged approximately 25 micrograms per 100 ml. Recent British researchers agree that similarly low blood-lead levels may be associated with mental retardation.[14] If correct, this means that hundreds of thousands of children in poverty areas affected by chipped lead paint, lead dust from industry, or lead-polluted air from automotive exhaust may be at great risk for sociocultural retardation. When it is realized that lead poisoning is only one environmental hazard present in areas of poverty, industrial blight, and deteriorated housing, the need to consider the physical environment as a significant source of sociocultural retardation becomes obvious and pressing.

MALNUTRITION

A pregnant mother's diet must provide the essential nutrients both for herself and her unborn child. When nutrition is deficient, the development of the child can be impaired. It is now generally accepted that malnutrition during fetal development or during the first eighteen months of life not only retards physical growth; it can cause mental retardation as well.[15] What is more, some experts believe that the mental retardation produced by malnutrition may be irreversible. The United Nations World Food Council declared in 1978 that 455 million of the world's people are malnourished and that one third of the world's children die before the age of five from malnutrition and related diseases. Severe malnutrition is not confined to war-ravaged countries such as Vietnam, Biafra, Bangladesh, or India. It also occurs in the Western nations. Recent surveys have shown that undernutrition is a widespread and serious problem in the United States, particularly among low-income black, Spanish-American, and American Indian populations.[16] We have already noted its presence in Appalachia.

Severe Malnutrition in Children. Severe malnutrition in children has been traditionally classified as either *infantile marasmus* or *kwashiorkor.* Marasmus is severe emaciation in a young child, usually under the age of two. It is caused by a very low intake of both calories and protein and results in extreme wasting of the body tissues. The child fails to grow and therefore appears very small for his age. Another striking feature of nutritional marasmus is the apathy and hyperirritability almost universally seen in these children. The more profound the caloric deprivation and the longer its duration, the worse its consequences, at least in terms of conventional clinical measurements, although even mild caloric deprivation in a young child will impair growth. Kwashiorkor is a syndrome marked by dry skin and skin rash, potbelly, edema, weakness, irritability, and gastrointestinal disturbances. It too results from a severe nutritional deficiency, particularly of protein.

Malnutrition is often accompanied by disease. Anemia is present more often than not, and diarrhea is very common, making the absorption of nutrients ineffective. Malnourished children are particularly susceptible to infection, and when infections occur they are far more serious than would be the case with normally nourished children. Gastrointestinal infections, typhus, and hepatitis are particularly common and serious, and severely undernourished children may have a death rate from measles as high as 50 percent.

But it is not simply that malnourished children are more susceptible to the effects of disease; they are also more often *exposed* to disease than are normal children. That is so because malnutrition is almost always associated with poverty and all of the related problems found in impoverished environments. For this reason it has been difficult to separate the effects of malnutrition from those of inadequate prenatal care, disease, cultural deprivation, large family size, lead poisoning, and a host of related factors.

In an effort to clarify the role of malnutrition in causing mental retardation, considerable research has been done with animals. For the most part this research indicates that malnourishment, especially low protein intake, does bring about reduced growth, small brain size, and impaired learning capacities. However, while animal research allows the investigator to control various environmental factors, such research is difficult to interpret because it is no simple matter to determine whether a rat is mentally retarded. Furthermore, there are some significant differences between animal and human development. As a result, animal experiments have not provided conclusive proof that early malnutrition alone causes mental retardation in humans.

There is also a considerable body of research with humans. Some of this research has focused on the survivors of periods of starvation, as occurred in Holland toward the end of World War II or more recently in Biafra. Other research has attempted to compare the mental development of severely malnourished children with children who have not suffered poor nutrition. The results of this research effort are again inconclusive. For one thing, severely malnourished children often do not survive; if they do live, they may not attend school, or they may be in a lower grade than would be normal for their age, thus putting them at a double disadvantage. What is more, the children with whom the malnourished children are compared are usually from higher socioeconomic strata in which not only nutrition but education and family life in general are far more favorable to mental development. Thus while study after study has found that malnourished children have retarded mental development when they are compared to better-nourished children, it is still difficult to determine to what extent this retardation is due to malnutrition rather than to other factors, including such subtle matters as lack of attention and motivation to learn.

Not surprisingly, research on malnutrition continues to be the subject of considerable debate. For example, leading researchers in this field, Myron Winick and his associates, attempted to determine what would happen if malnourished children from poor socioeconomic backgrounds were raised in households in substantially higher socioeconomic strata.[17] Winick's research group studied Korean orphans who had been subjected to various degrees of malnutrition in Korea before being adopted by middle-class American families. The mean age of these children was eighteen months at the time of adoption, and they were in elementary school in the United States when Winick studied them. Their adoptive parents had no knowledge of the previous nutritional status of the children.

The results are in striking contrast to those obtained from studies of similar groups of children who returned to the environments in which they were originally malnourished. For example, even the severely malnourished adopted Korean children had surpassed Korean norms of height and weight. Moreover, the marked initial size differences between the malnourished and the well-nourished infants had almost entirely disappeared. Perhaps even more striking is the fact that the mean IQ of the severely malnourished children is 102. This is higher than the mean IQ of middle-class American children, and it is about 40 points higher than the mean IQ reported for similarly malnourished children who remained in their early home environments. In addition, achievement in school for the severely malnourished group was found to be equal to that expected of normal American children. But, as Winick notes, the stigmata of malnutrition had not entirely disappeared by the time these children were studied. Thus there continue to be significant differences between the previously malnourished and well-nourished Korean children in IQ and school achievement scores. Whether these are permanent differences it is too early to tell.

Another careful study, this time in Sri Lanka, raises further questions. J. P. Das and P. Soysa compared 42 children who had been hospitalized for marasmus and kwashiorkor six to seven years earlier with a group of children from their own nieghborhood, matched on age and sex.[18] None of the latter children had been hospitalized for malnutrition. In addition, 33 siblings of the hospitalized children were compared with age-and sex-matched neighborhood children. Thus Das and Soysa were able to compare severely malnourished children with undernourished children from the same socioeconomic background. In comparing the cognitive functions of these groups the researchers found no differences that could be related to malnutrition. They concluded that an episode of severe malnutrition may do no more harm than chronic undernutrition. However, they did find a strong relationship between mental ability and years of schooling. Das and Soysa suggest that even for these disadvantaged children—all of whom were both undernourished and raised in an extremely deprived environment—school attendance can markedly improve the child's intellectual performance.

Another approach has involved supplementation of the diet of malnourished mothers and young children. This research has shown that malnourished children quickly respond to a normal diet by being more active physically, smiling more, and becoming more verbal. However, clear-cut evidence that the intellectual abilities of these children have risen has been difficult to produce.

A recent study has produced some important results. Harrison McKay and his colleagues placed groups of chronically under-nourished preschool age children from Cali, Colombia, in a pro-gram that combined nutritional supplementation with health care and educational instruction.[19] These children were put into several groups representing a range of nutritional and socio-economic deprivation. Five of the groups were malnourished children from low socioeconomic-status families; each group received a different number or kind of treatment. One group was well nourished from high socioeconomic-status families; this group was untreated, as was a group of low socioeconomic-status children who were not undernourished.

An average treatment day consisted of six hours of integrated health, nutritional, and educational activities, in which approxi-mately four hours were devoted to education and two hours to health, nutrition, and hygiene. The nutritional supplementation program was designed to provide a minimum of 75 percent of recommended daily protein and calorie allowances by means of low-cost foods available commercially, supplemented with vita-mins and minerals, and offered three times a day. The health care program included daily observation of all children attending the treatment center, with immediate medical attention to those with symptoms reported by the parents or noted by the health and education personnel. The educational treatment was de-signed to employ an integrated curriculum model in order to develop cognitive abilities and language, social abilities, and psychomotor skills.

The results leave little doubt that environmental deprivation of a degree severe enough to produce chronic undernutrition re-tards general intellectual development, and that this retardation is more resistant to modification with increasing age. Neverthe-less, the study shows that combined nutritional, health, and edu-cational treatments between three and a half and seven years of age can prevent large losses of potential intellectual ability. The earlier the treatments begin, the greater is the effect. As little as nine months of treatment prior to primary school appears to produce significant increases in ability, although these gains are small compared to those of children receiving treatment lasting two, three, and four times as long. Continued study will be necessary to ascertain the long-range persistence of these gains, but the present data show that they persist at eight years of age. The authors conclude:

> The increases in general cognitive ability produced by the multiform preschool interventions are socially significant in that they reduce the large intelligence gap between children from severely deprived environments and those from favored environments, although the extent to which any given amount of intervention might be beneficial to wider societal development is uncertain. Extrapolated to the large number of children throughout the world who spend their first years in poverty and hunger, however, even the smallest increment resulting from one 9-month treatment period could constitute an important improvement in the pool of human capabilities available to a given society.[20]

Thus it still is not clear how much malnutrition alone contributes to sociocultural retardation. But it is clear that when nutrition is improved along with other crucial aspects of a child's environment, such as health and education, that even early malnutrition need not lead to permanent mental retardation. We must not lose sight of the fact that malnutrition rarely occurs in a social or cultural vacuum. With rare exceptions, it is a part of a larger poverty complex. As we have seen, schooling may be even more important than good nutrition in reducing the incidence of sociocultural retardation.

THE SCHOOLS

It may seem strange to think of schools as one of the causes of sociocultural retardation, but a number of experts assert exactly this. They make the claim because most socioculturally retarded children are first officially identified as such in school, and once these children leave school many will never be identified as retarded again. In the United States, this phenomenon has led to the use of the term "the six-hour retarded child," referring to the fact that children who cannot adequately perform the academic tests required in school nevertheless adapt perfectly well to life outside school. Thus the argument has been made that since these children who are primarily poor, minority-group members from inner cities are only retarded in school, then the school itself has "created" their retardation.

We know that some children who are identified as socioculturally retarded in school are not completely competent outside school, but since the great majority of socioculturally retarded children are both poor and from culturally different backgrounds, the possibility remains that schools are treating these children as if they were mentally retarded when in reality they are simply unprepared—in terms of language, culture, or motivation—to cope effectively with the academic demands that schools place upon them.

What is the evidence? In a well-known study, sociologist Jane Mercer found that school psychologists in Riverside, California, were more likely to recommend poor or Mexican-American children for placement in special classes for the mentally retarded than they were other children who had the same IQ.[21] In an earlier study in Missouri children who were diagnosed as having a learning disability (which means a child of *normal* intelligence who for one or another reason has difficulty learning at a normal pace) were 96.8 percent Caucasian; yet black children were found to constitute 34.2 percent of the children placed in classes for the educable mentally retarded (EMR).[22] A similar discrepancy was found in Scotland, where it was reported that middle-class children of the same IQ as poorer children tended to be placed in classes for children with minimal brain injuries (MBI); the poorer children were classified as mentally retarded and were placed in classes for the educably subnormal.[23]

These studies and others like them show that the unfairness found in school classifications and special-class placement is not solely or even primarily a result of the unfairness inherent in IQ tests themselves. Nevertheless, there *can* be unfairness in the use of IQ tests with culturally disadvantaged children, as recent court decisions in the United States have affirmed. For example, because it was found that ethnic minority children who had been placed in special classes for the mentally retarded scored on an average of 15 points higher when given an IQ test in their native language, a court ruled (*Diana v. California State Board of Education*) that all children must be tested in their native language prior to placement in special classes, that all Mexican-American and Chinese-American children in special classes be relocated, and that a new, more culturally fair means of assessment be developed and standardized.

It is important to keep in mind here that we are referring only to socioculturally retarded children. Clinically retarded children (often referred to as TMR or trainable mentally retarded) are often badly in need of special education, which some school districts have been either unable or unwilling to provide. Recent court decisions have made it mandatory that *all* children requiring special education be sought out and that services appropriate to their needs be provided.

It does not seem to be the case that very many teachers or school psychologists have been intentionally unfair to poor or culturally different children. To be sure, stereotypes and prejudices may sometimes be at work, but the process by which one child rather than another becomes identified as mentally retarded is usually both complex and subtle. First, socioculturally retarded children are seldom identified in school primarily on the basis of the IQ test. Instead, they first come to attention because they fail in the classroom. This failure leads the teacher to seek psychological evaluation, which may include psychological testing. As various studies have shown, the decision whether to place a child in some sort of specialized class for mentally retarded students is a complex one, and many students, poor and ethnic minorities as well as middle-class, remain in regular classes.

A second fundamental issue is whether children who cannot succeed academically and who have low IQs are better served by being placed in a special class with other children who have similar problems or by leaving them in the regular classroom. There has been an enormous outpouring of research on this issue, most of which is badly flawed. There is still great controversy about which course of action is better. Part of the problem is that what is best for one retarded child may not be best for another.

The current trend in the United States is "mainstreaming"—placing retarded children in regular classes with nonretarded children for all or most of the school day. This approach came about because of the widespread belief that retarded children made slower progress in special classes than they did in regular ones. A crucial test of this issue came about in California in 1969. Civil rights advocates had charged that placement in EMR classes was based on the use of IQ tests that were biased against students from ethnic minority groups; they pointed out that whereas black and Spanish-surname children comprised only 24.1 percent of the total school population in California, they were 55.3 percent of all EMR students. As a result, a series of legislative acts attempted to correct this situation, ordering that all children in EMR classes be reassessed with "nonbiased" tests. EMR enrollments were reduced in California by as much as 18,000 over the next few years, and these children were mainstreamed into regular classes.

This massive experiment in mainstreaming did not occur under conditions that allowed careful consideration to be given to the needs of each child. Instead, the decision to mainstream a child was made in large measure on the basis of an IQ test score —the very test score that had led to the civil rights action in the first place. This objection notwithstanding, mainstreaming did take place and its results are worth examining. As reported by Donald MacMillan, three groups of children were compared: (1) children formerly in EMR classes who had been returned to regular classes (the mainstream or M group), (2) children in EMR classes who were not mainstreamed (the EMR group), and (3) low-achieving regular class students in the same classes in which the mainstreamed children were enrolled (the RC group).[24]

The first major finding was that the M children were doing surprisingly well academically. On the average they were achieving above the level of the EMR children, and at a level comparable to that of the RC children. Moreover, contrary to the common fear, the pressures of regular class did not cause the children to drop out of school more often than EMR children did. Teachers rated the social acceptance of the M students to be a little below average, but a considerable range was reported with some M students being positively accepted in regular class. In general, the M students were rated as having the same pattern of acceptance as RC children.

MacMillan also reports that 29 percent of the regular-class teachers indicated that they took no extra measures to accommodate the M students. These students were not seen as being disruptive or as posing a problem in class; they were perceived instead as marginal students of low ability, like the low-achieving RC children. However, EMR teachers were pessimistic about the academic and social success of the mainstreamed children; significantly, they complained that the mainstreaming program had removed from their EMR classes some of their own best helpers. These contrastive teacher reactions and expectations may illustrate what many have suspected about special classes—the expectations of EMR class teachers for their students may be too low, leading to self-fulfilling low achievement. These students may do better in regular classes where teacher expectations are somewhat higher.

Much more research needs to be done, in California and elsewhere, before any firm conclusions can be reached, but the California mainstreaming experiment seems to indicate what so many critics of special-class placement have been saying—placing low-achieving, low-IQ children in special classes may well be doing them a disservice. As Binet and Simon, pioneers of special education for the retarded and of IQ testing, said in 1905: "It will never be to one's credit to have attended a special school. We should at least spare from this mark those who do not deserve it."

While disagreement and sometimes bitter dispute will continue, there is general agreement on one point: schools should assess the individual needs of their students and provide programs that best meet the needs of children, whatever the handicaps or disabilities may be. As MacMillan has put it, after each retarded child has been assessed, he should be placed in a program that is as close to regular classroom education as his personal needs and abilities permit. These programs should be designed so that retarded children can be integrated into regular education in a way that is beneficial for retarded and nonretarded children alike. Furthermore, the needs and abilities of retarded children should be reassessed frequently to assure that every child is receiving the best possible education in terms of his or her changing needs and characteristics.

7 / After Schooling

Although retarded people may be thought of and even referred to as children throughout their lives, like the rest of us they grow older and, also like the rest of us, they must confront the challenges of being adults. When socioculturally retarded persons leave school, usually at about age eighteen, they begin to face the adult challenges. Where will they live? Can they earn a living? Will they marry and raise children? What can they look forward to in life?

Today very few socioculturally retarded persons are placed in large institutions. Most begin their adult lives in their parents' homes. Some remain there, but many soon move to a group home or hostel where they live with other handicapped persons under varying degrees of supervision. Others live independently, moving into their own residences and managing their lives with little or no assistance.

A great amount of research has been undertaken in an effort to learn how well socioculturally retarded persons are able to take on the responsibilities of adult living. This research consistently reports that a very large proportion of the adult retarded manage to achieve a satisfactory adjustment to community life. Although such persons often have difficulties in the early years of their adult lives, after a period of time they seem to do surprisingly well.[1] In fact, the community adjustment of mildly retarded adults is usually so successful that many of them—perhaps as many as half—who were once officially labeled as retarded disappear from official note altogether. Such people neither seek nor receive any services as mentally retarded. It is presumed that such people have been absorbed into normal community life.[2]

Study after study shows that while it is impossible to predict which personal or intellectual characteristics are necessary for successful community adjustment (the IQ of a socioculturally retarded person has consistently *failed* to predict the success of adult adjustment), we can nevertheless predict that the majority of socioculturally retarded adults will make a satisfactory adjustment to community life. That is, they do not get into trouble with the authorities and they meet the demands of their particular environment with normal adult behavior. Although most research shows that socioculturally retarded adults do not do as well economically as normal people from a similar socioeconomic background, it is nonetheless the case that many of the retarded are able to live apparently normal lives, including marriage and, sometimes, having children.

Perhaps the best available example of a long-term study of community adjustment of socioculturally retarded adults is a thirty-year study of people who as children had been identified as mentally retarded in the public schools of Lincoln, Nebraska.[3] In comparing these socioculturally retarded people with nonretarded classmates, Baller, Charles, and Miller found that the retarded persons eventually made a reasonably good social adjustment, including the ability on the part of the majority to be self-supporting. However, the early years of their adjustment were turbulent and difficult. The researchers account for the eventual success of these people as follows:

> One answer is *time*—they had to learn from experience in society rather than in the home. This necessity forced a slow and fumbling start, and much experience of failure. This "slow start" was reflected in the records of many subjects whose adolescent and early adult years were marked by delinquency, dependency on relief, and generally poor adjustment but whose later adult lives were reasonably satisfactory.[4]

Some studies report that satisfactory adjustment can occur without an initial period of social failure. For example, Anne-Marie Henschel reported that a fairly good and stable adjustment was made by socioculturally retarded people of both

Anglo- and Mexican-American descent in Texas.[5] A recent study by Stephen Richardson of a city in Scotland has produced even more positive findings.[6] Richardson compared all individuals aged twenty-two who had once been classified mentally retarded in that city. He matched these socioculturally retarded young adults with normal people of the same sex, age, and social background. At age twenty-two, two thirds of the retarded persons were not receiving any special mental retardation services. Of these only 8 percent were unemployed, as compared to 2 percent of the "normal" comparison population. This is a remarkable rate of employment, but it should be kept in mind that this study was conducted at a time of almost full employment for this age group and, what is more, the retarded people had jobs that required fewer skills, less take-home pay, and fewer dealings with the public. In addition, as compared to the normal controls, fewer of the retarded were married, fewer had a close friend of the opposite sex, and fewer said that they felt that they had got along well with other people since leaving school.

The economic success of retarded people is obviously related to the economy as a whole, and the retarded, who have few marketable skills, are especially vulnerable to economic recession. Yet their marital stability, which is less vulnerable to external social forces, is usually reported to be quite high. Thus although socioculturally retarded women are more likely to marry than are retarded men, once retarded individuals marry, their marriages often endure and appear to be happy. For example, Janet Mattinson studied thirty-six British couples who had married following their release from an institution for the mentally retarded. Only four of these thirty-six marriages were not being maintained seven years later. Mattinson judged twenty-five of these marriages to be affectionate.[7] Similar findings have been reported in the United States.

Parental success is both more controversial and difficult to assess. For one thing, socioculturally retarded parents have a higher likelihood of giving birth to a retarded child than do normal parents. For another, even if the child should have a normal IQ, as is sometimes the case, the home environment that the retarded parents can offer their child is often less than optimal. A child can be both an economic and a psychological burden for retarded parents. As a result, many socioculturally retarded parents need help with child care, or must relinquish their child altogether.[8] We shall return to this complex subject again when we consider mental retardation as a societal problem. For now it is enough to note that although socioculturally retarded people often have stable and rewarding marriages, their role as parents is a good deal more problematic.

A CLOSER LOOK AT COMMUNITY LIVING

Thus far we have been speaking in generalities and, however true these general statements may be, they gloss the realities of the everyday lives of socioculturally retarded people. My own research with the people released from a large state hospital for the retarded has continued since 1960.[9] When I first studied these people in 1960 they were consumed by feelings of shame at being hospitalized as mentally retarded. As a result they devoted themselves to denying the correctness of this label and to passing as nonretarded. Many of these persons had obvious doubts about their right to claim to be normal, since they chose to deceive others about their past institutionalization and their abilities. For example, they pretended to be able to read, write, tell time, and drive, and they displayed fraudulent memorabilia in an effort to reconstruct a normal past life.

Twelve years later, concern with shame and passing was far less evident. No longer was it one of the first or more recurrent themes of conversation. In 1960 I concluded that in general, the ex-patient succeeds in his efforts to sustain a life in the community only as well as he succeeds in locating and holding a "benefactor."[10] For most of these former patients, benefactors provided vital assistance with life's crises, as well as with more routine aspects of everyday life. In many cases, benefactors were also important resources in the process of coping with shame and in passing as normal. Twelve years later, however, benefactors appeared to play a less important role in all these respects. This change could have been brought about either by a lesser need for benefactors or by a lesser availability of them. In any event, it is no longer possible to say that the adaptive success of these people is primarily a function of their relation to benefactors. Why this change has come about is not entirely clear, but it seems likely that the reduced impact of stigma has helped to lessen the need for benefactors and that another twelve years of experience in community living has also reduced the need for assistance with everyday problems or crises.

Vocational success has commonly been regarded as an essential feature of social adjustment. S. Olshansky has succinctly reflected the prevailing opinion: "While intellectuals may debate the passing of the protestant ethic, and while for them, work may not be as meaningful as in past decades, the fact is that for many disabled persons suffering intellectual, physical, or emotional limitations, work serves as one of the central facts of their lives."[11] In 1960 many of the former patients clearly accepted work as the quintessential means of proving themselves to be normal, worthy human beings.

In order to qualify for vocational leave from Pacific State Hospital, these people had to demonstrate their abilities to perform well on the job, and at the time of discharge, all of these people were employed in the community. Twelve years later, most of them were unemployed. For one thing, the economy had worsened markedly since 1960 and, for another, it may have been easier to qualify for welfare payments. But twelve years of aging also took its toll on these unskilled workers. Their average age twelve years later was forty-seven—not yet superannuated but no longer a favorable age for unskilled persons to be competing for jobs. More significant perhaps is the increased physical disability that had gone along with aging. In 1960 they were in good health, with only a few troubled by any chronic illness or serious injury. Twelve years later, half of these people remained in excellent health, but the rest had various ailments, and nine others were disabled. These older and more infirm persons made repeated comments to the effect that they could no longer be expected to work and that welfare checks were a perfectly satisfactory, and deserved, source of income. This is, of course, an attitude also expressed by people in the general population.[12]

Twelve years later, what we heard from these people and what we observed from being around them was a vital interest in enjoying life. What seemed to dominate their interests was not work or shame or passing, but recreation, hobbies, leisure, good times, friends, and family. There was no particular evidence of alienation from work of the kind Studs Terkel so vividly documented for some Americans,[13] but only a preoccupation with things other than work. They had become geared to enjoying life, and most of them had quite convincingly relegated work to a purely instrumental role. Many of these people had developed varied and rewarding styles of life, involving many friends, activities, and pastimes. Even several of the relatively isolated members of the cohort led lives that they found interesting and pleasurable. For example, a fifty-eight-year-old woman who was widowed in 1963 lived alone, supported by welfare payments. She could have developed a reclusive way of life, relying on her television set for stimulation, but instead she spent time in her garden, enjoyed her dog and bird, and maintained her small house very carefully. She devoted most of her time to creative hobbies such as painting and candlemaking and was quite skilled at both. Her neighbor was a friend, not a benefactor. In all, hers was a satisfying, even creative, way of life.

That the lives of these socioculturally retarded people were, in the main, more varied and pleasurable in 1972 than in 1960 is not our inference alone. We asked each individual to compare his or her life to a period "about ten years ago." In terms of expressed happiness, even though employment had declined since 1960, most people said that they were as happy, or happier, in 1972 than they were before. Nothing that we observed gave us reason to doubt that what they said was sincere.

That successful community adjustment is complex is by now a truism, but it is by no means generally accepted that successful community adjustment may be independent of vocational success. Yet, if the experiences and feelings of these persons are at all instructive, that is the conclusion we must reach. We have already seen that the majority of them felt happier later in life than they did before, and that their happiness was not a function of employment. What is more, many of these people now appear to define themselves as "normal" despite their lack of vocational success.

DECEPTIONS, FICTIONS, REALITIES

Before we go any further, it is important to note that existing knowledge about the lives of retarded people in the community is quite superficial. Most of the published information we possess is based on interviews with socioculturally retarded people themselves, or with their parents, employers, or social workers. Little of what is published is based on direct observation of their lives. The resulting information can easily be downright inaccurate. In particular, this information fails adequately to convey the complexity and the fluctuation of these lives.

My own research with my colleagues has attempted to supplement existing information by the use of intensive first-hand study, requiring years spent getting to know retarded people and participating in most aspects of their lives. In this research we become, if only relatively so, a "natural" part of their lives. When we succeed, and sometimes we do not, we eventually gain access to more than the public domain of their lives. We assume that retarded people, and those normal people who are involved in one or another aspect of their lives, say and do many things in order to present a favorable face to others. Our ethnographic procedures are attuned to this Janus-faced quality of self-presentation, and by virtue of our prolonged and somewhat unpredictable presence in their world, we hope to be able to see more than the obvious. We drop by, we take retarded persons away from their residences, and we stay in their residences overnight or for a week or more. We attend important events in the lives of these people, going to weddings, family gatherings, or weekend outings, and we introduce them to new recreational experiences. We videotape many of these encounters so that we and the participants themselves can discuss and interpret the behavior that took place (we also erase the videotapes if these people find anything in them that is objectionable). Our procedures do not "break down" all deception—efforts to deceive are an important part of the reality we try to study—nor do they reduce the complexities of human life to clear and simple truths. However, they do lessen the likelihood that an obvious deception will go unnoticed and that the contradictory complexity of a human life, even a "retarded" life, will be seen as simple and straightforward. The method is not intended to provide simple answers; it is intended to provide the empirical grounds for rejecting simple answers in favor of fuller and more accurate understanding.[14]

By applying these procedures, month after month, we are often able to separate fiction from reality as, for example, when group home caregivers speak as if they had the best interests of their retarded residents at heart when, in fact, observation of their behavior makes it clear that their own self-interest is uppermost. Sometimes, too, we can detect the deceptions of mentally retarded people who often attempt to deceive parents, social workers, or caregivers. We have often witnessed highly compelling performances in which a socioculturally retarded person succeeds in convincing his or her social worker that some outrageous lie is the absolute truth. For example, we witnessed an impressive performance by a man who was attempting to convince his social worker that he was sufficiently competent to be married. This he did by displaying to the surprised social worker a valid driver's license for his new motorcycle. Mel was a thirty-five-year-old whose IQ was 55. His left arm was badly withered as a result of childhood polio. He could neither read nor write, and at times he appeared much less intelligent than his IQ would indicate. He had absolutely no ability to understand numbers, a problem that left him almost completely unable to use money. He had bought the motorcycle with the assistance of normal friends who dealt with the problems of money and insurance for him. However, Mel got a driver's license on his own after being told that there were only five versions of the written examination. Although he scored only a few correct answers on his first exam, the examiner routinely marked the errors on the answer sheet. Mel concluded that he would try again, surreptitiously matching his first answer sheet to each new exam, until he encountered the same form and scored 100 percent correct. This he did on his fourth try. When he presented his license and motorcycle to the social worker, he gave her to understand that the motorcycle purchase and the acquisition of the driver's license were accomplished solely on his own, facts to demonstrate his competence to marry. She gave her approval and he married. The marriage lasted three weeks and was not consummated.

But it is not only social workers who can be gulled. We, too, can be deceived, even after a year or more of almost continuous contact with a retarded person. Jim was a young man of twenty-five with an IQ of about 70; he was quite handsome and articulate, giving every impression of being a perfectly normal young man. He enhanced this impression by his frequent, fully appropriate use of sexually tinged innuendo, including the adroit use of double entendre. He seemed to be a sexually sophisticated man who was familiar with all the nuances and complexities of sexuality. We remained convinced that this was so for a full year, and it was only through chance that we discovered that he was in actuality so ignorant of the facts of sexuality that he believed that people had sexual intercourse solely in order to procreate. He was unaware of the presumably self-evident fact that sexual intercourse can be physically pleasurable. He was so ignorant of the sensual side of sexuality that he did not even understand why people might masturbate. Despite this monumental misunderstanding of the basic nature of sexual feeling, he had been able to convince us and others that he was altogether knowledgeable about sexual matters. Needless to say, other socioculturally retarded persons have continued to deceive us about more subtle aspects of life.

The point is not simply that socioculturally retarded persons can and do deceive others about their beliefs and fears and basic competence. Like normal people, they are complex human beings and they lead complex lives. We have spent years trying to understand those lives, only to realize that we always fall far short of full understanding. For example, for almost eighteen years we have been attempting to understand the life of one man with an IQ in the 50s. There is much about his life in that period that we still do not fathom, and there is much about him as a person that remains contradictory and puzzling. But that should hardly surprise us since all people have contradictory and somewhat unpredictable lives. It only becomes an issue because professionals make such far-reaching decisions about the welfare of mentally retarded people on the basis of partial and superficial information. It is as if professionals have deceived themselves into believing that retarded people lead simple lives. They do not.

It is equally important to realize that the lives of socioculturally retarded people are highly changeable, not just in mood or happiness but in the most fundamental aspects, such as self-esteem, employment, marriage, and general social competence. In studies of the mentally retarded that have utilized normal comparison populations, it is often reported that the lives of the retarded are somewhat more unstable than those of nonretarded people, but that greater stability emerges as they spend more time in community living. This pattern may typify some retarded people, but many whom we have studied seem to experience continued instability in their lives no matter what their age or how long they have lived independently.

This may be so because most mentally retarded people have few reliable resources that can stabilize them in times of crisis. With no job security, few marketable skills, and no network of reliable friends or relatives, the loss of a job, benefactor, or spouse can precipitate a major change in their level of adaptation. Most of these socioculturally retarded people would seem to have only a tenuous control over their life circumstances. As a result their lives are probably more unpredictable than those of people who control essential aspects of their lives through savings, job security, retirement plans, health insurance, and networks of friends and relatives.

Time after time our research with socioculturally retarded adults who live in various community settings has recorded the most abrupt and traumatic changes in basic life circumstances. It is a minority whose lives remain on an even keel for as much as a year at a time. For the rest it is common to see major changes in place of residence, jobs, personal relationships, marriages, emotional stability, and self-esteem. In our experience, quite a few of these young adults can be expected to suffer severe psychological stress, sometimes requiring hospitalization, as a result of a divorce, the loss of a job, or the failure to achieve some major goal in life. Normal people suffer acute stress as a reaction to such crises too, but for the retarded these changes are usually more consequential because other people—parents, social workers, caregivers, and the like—make decisions for them based on what they know at one particular point in time. Because the level of competence or general adaptation seen at any given point in time is almost certain to change, any decision made is likely to be mistaken. Retarded people who are coping very well one month will probably not cope well a month later, and even those who have hit bottom and are fully dependent and incompetent at one point in time can be markedly better in a few months.

The experiences of Mary and Louise illustrate this pattern of events. Both women were twenty-four years old when we first encountered them. Although each was socioculturally retarded with an IQ close to 70, they were living in a group home in which all the other residents were clinically retarded, sometimes severely so. Not only was this group home a terribly unstimulating environment for these young women, it was a highly restrictive one as well. They were denied the right to leave the facility for any reason except to visit a sheltered workshop where they performed the monotonous task of sorting variously sized screws into containers. Contrary to state regulations, they could not have visitors at this facility except for their parents, who seldom visited since they lived several hundred miles away. They were even denied access to a telephone. Each night they were reduced to watching television and, heavily tranquilized, going to sleep early. Because this vegetative life seemed so contrary to their best interests and abilities, and because they were being tranquilized into near stupor by the caregiver, our research staff, with medical advice, intervened and moved them to a group home where they could be given an opportunity to learn to live as much as possible like normal young women.

Mary and Louise were delighted with their newfound freedom but, sadly and dramatically, they were unprepared to behave appropriately in so unsupervised a setting. Mary, who was an extremely attractive young woman, discovered boyfriends for the first time. The residence and the nearby neighborhood abounded with young men and Mary seemingly invited all of them into bed, often more than one at a time. When her lovemaking became too noisy or too public, other residents would complain, but Mary seemed unable to confine her sexual activities to appropriate times, places, or people. On one particularly traumatic occasion, she was discovered by the police having sexual intercourse in a large metal trash container behind a nearby supermarket. At this point, the temptation to return Mary to a more restricted environment was considerable, to say the least. Everyone forebore, however, and explained to her again and again what was and was not acceptable sexual conduct. After a few months, she learned. Needless to say, she has encountered other problems in adapting to an unfamiliar life of near normalcy, but her sexual misconduct has disappeared and in general she has continued to make progress toward a more normal life.

Louise experienced another sort of difficulty. She was quite good with numbers, so her new caregiver lent her a pocket electronic calculator and taught her various things about keeping records for the facility, among which was the practice of writing checks. Louise soon discovered that if a check for $7 from a sheltered workshop had a 5 placed in front of the 7, it would be worth substantially more. She made such changes and attempted to cash several of these altered checks at a nearby liquor store. Fortunately, the store owner knew how much a workshop check should be worth and did not cash them; even more fortunate, he did not call the police. In a short time, Louise also learned what was acceptable and did not repeat her experiments in forgery. But had someone intervened at this point in her life, she could well have been returned to a restricted environment where she could not get into such trouble. She will undoubtedly get into further trouble before she learns at the age of twenty-four what most women learn about life ten years earlier. In the main, however, she has greatly improved her level of adaptation in her new environment.

Those who read about the lives of the mentally retarded would do well to be skeptical about information that does not take into account the complex changes in the lives of these people.

It seems to be the case that many, perhaps even most, socioculturally retarded adults can make some sort of satisfactory adjustment to community living. As time goes on many will improve their social competence, their independence, and the overall quality of their lives. Most can work productively when unskilled or semiskilled jobs are available, and few will find themselves in serious trouble with the law. Many will marry and have a responsible and happy domestic existence; some will be good parents, but most will probably have difficulty with this role. Parenthood is a serious question for these people and for society, and we still know far too little about the capabilities of socioculturally retarded people as parents.

Many of these people will disappear from the sight of officials and agencies who provide services to the mentally retarded. We do not know whether this is so because they have become sufficiently competent to get along without support, whether they fear recognition by official agencies, or whether they are simply ignorant of the availability of such resources. It seems likely that all these factors operate. Some retarded people, such as Afro-

Americans or Mexican-Americans, may disappear from official view because they have the support of large extended families, a resource not available to most retarded people from Anglo-American backgrounds.

What kind of lives mentally retarded people can live and how much help they need to lead rewarding and productive lives are questions that transcend the personal concerns of retarded people and their parents. These are questions of significance for all of us, for society itself, and we shall consider them next.

8/ Some Implications for Society

The existence of mental retardation, particularly sociocultural retardation, poses many problems for society. We shall consider some of the most basic ones, beginning with the current practice of "normalization."

THE SHIFT FROM INSTITUTION TO COMMUNITY

In the United States and in Britain, government has made a policy of normalization mandatory. This means making available to mentally retarded people conditions of everyday life that are as nearly normal as possible. As a result, legislation has been passed providing that the mentally retarded are entitled to receive needed services under the least restrictive, most normal circumstances possible. In addition, each retarded individual is to be given every opportunity to be integrated into community living—in an ideal sense, this means regular employment, regular schooling, and independent living arrangements. It also means dignity and privacy. The principle of normalization does not presume that every retarded person is capable of fully normal living; for many clinically retarded persons such normalcy can never be achieved. Instead, normalization aims toward helping each individual achieve a way of life that is *nearly* normal.

If we are to understand normalization, we must first understand the history of institutional treatment of retarded persons. Before the middle of the nineteenth century, mentally retarded people in the United States and Great Britain were cared for by their families, or in local communities. The treatment they received was sometimes loving, other times brutal and dehumanizing. The first large institutions for the mentally retarded were founded not only on humanitarian grounds but in the belief that the retarded could be educated and returned to their communities. This experiment failed, and the result was a widespread movement toward the end of the nineteenth century to build larger, custodial institutions which would provide life-long protection against the evils and dangers of society. For this period one can read again and again of the need to protect retarded women against "rapacious and brutal" men, and retarded men against the numberless vices of the outside world.

Around the turn of the century, especially in the United States, there was a marked change in public sentiment. Now it was society that needed to be protected against the mentally retarded, about whom there were hysterical public pronouncements decrying their criminality and immorality. These comments by responsible, even scholarly citizens were typical of those times:

> When we view the number of the feebleminded, their fecundity, their lack of control, the menace they are, the degradation they cause, the degeneracy they perpetuate, the suffering and misery and crime they spread,—these are the burdens we must bear.[1]

Retarded girls came in for especially virulent attacks:

> There is probably no class of persons who are more fitted and more apt to spread disease and moral evil than these girls.[2]

From our contemporary perspective of commitment to normalization, it is difficult to comprehend the public alarm about retardation that existed earlier in this century. For example, Walter E. Fernald was one of the most influential persons in the United States in the field of mental retardation. There are still schools for the retarded that bear his name. These are some of his published comments about the mentally retarded:

> The modern American community is very intolerant of the presence of these dangerous defectives with the desires and passions of adult life, without control of reason or judgment. There

is a widespread and insistent demand that these women be put under control . . . the adult males become the town loafers and incapables, the irresponsible pests of the neighborhood, petty thieves, purposeless destroyers of property, incendiaries, and very frequently violators of women and little girls.[3]

British Royal Commission reports in 1908 and 1915 echoed these sentiments, referring to the "absolute and urgent necessity" of dealing with this "evil of the very greatest magnitude."

This "evil" was dealt with by consigning increasing numbers of mildly retarded adults to state-operated institutions where they were expected to remain for the rest of their lives. The institutions themselves clearly reflected the purposes for which they were intended. They were separated from the community by their isolated rural locations, and they were frequently fenced in with locked living areas and barred windows. The sexes were segregated in large, barren dormitories. The buildings and furnishings were built of unbreakable materials; in recent years, television sets and light fixtures were still protected by screens. The staff was isolated behind screens or windows where they could observe the inmates without personal contact. There was no privacy in bedrooms, showers, or toilets—all were open spaces that were frequently observed by staff and even visitors. Inmates were expected to work in institutional farms or factories to help defray the cost of their custody.

Such institutions continued to house large numbers of retarded people of all kinds—sociocultural as well as clinical—through the 1950s. Beginning about that time, there was a shift in policy away from custodial confinement and toward a more therapeutic orientation. This transformation was speeded by the influence of Scandinavian models of deinstitutionalized care and normalization. Knowledge of Swedish and Danish patterns of care in small community-based hotels or group homes spread while John F. Kennedy, as president of the United States, exerted his considerable personal efforts on behalf of the mentally retarded. As the British and Americans began to consider shifting mentally retarded residents of large institutions to small, home-like residences with more normal living conditions, they began to "discover" that conditions in their state institutions were deplorable. Reports of horrible conditions proliferated in both countries. The following report about conditions in a large institution in the United States by the President's Committee on Mental Retardation is but one of hundreds like it:

> The seclusion rooms are small cells with locked doors, barred windows, and are just large enough for one bed and a mattress on the floor. Residents are locked in these rooms without supervision and for long periods of time.
>
> One resident who was recently observed in a seclusion room had been there as long as the ward attendant had been assigned to that ward, which was six years. Physical restraints, including straight jackets, nylon stockings, rags as well as rope, are often used without physician's orders. One young girl was observed in a straight jacket, tied to a wooden bench. It was explained that she sucked her fingers and had been so restrained for nine years.[4]

Not all large institutions were characterized by neglect or abuse of their inmates; some offered quite positive and therapeutic care for at least certain of their residents. Nevertheless, by the middle of the 1960s an exodus from these institutions to various smaller community residential arrangements was well under way, and it is still continuing. There are reports that emphasize the success of this process of deinstitutionalization, pointing to improved social relationships, more varied life experiences, better job performance, and much improved social independence. However, other studies, especially in the United States and Canada, report that life in these community residential settings can be more restrictive and less normalized than was the case in large institutions.

The problems in these small residential facilities commonly include the pairing of severely retarded residents with mildly retarded ones, poor medical treatment including the use of medication to control behavior, restrictive attitudes held by untrained staffs, and isolation from community activities. In general, while there is evidence here and there that exciting progress toward normalization is being made, for most mentally retarded people life in community residential settings has proven to be no more normal than it was in large institutions, and for some it is even more restrictive.[5]

Normalization is policy, not just philosophy, and the years to come will undoubtedly witness continuing efforts to provide mentally retarded persons with the opportunity for more nearly normal lives. As progress is made toward this goal, there are several problem areas that are likely to continue to cause social tensions and to thwart the realization of normalization. The first of these involves sexuality. When the retarded were first isolated from society, one of the main justifications was their alleged inability to protect themselves against sexual predators; when society was being "protected" against the retarded, the rapacious sexuality of these people was greatly feared. For example, as recently as the 1960s, many states compelled retarded people in institutions to be surgically sterilized before they could be released from confinement, and the majority of the states still have laws prohibiting the mentally retarded from marrying. These laws are usually unenforced, but sexuality nevertheless remains an issue. Socioculturally retarded adults are still subject to subtle and not so subtle coercion to undergo sterilization before they marry, and there is considerable resistance on the part of parents and the public at large to the idea that mentally retarded people should enjoy sexual relations with as much freedom as normal persons do. And we have already noticed the widespread concern that such people will not make adequate parents. Normalization must include normal sexuality, including the right to bear children. Thus far, however, these rights have been withheld from many retarded people.

Another potential point of social concern involves work. As we have seen, most proponents of normalization regard work as an essential step toward becoming normal. But as we have also seen, many physically capable, mildly retarded adults are unable to find employment and others would far rather receive welfare allotments than do tedious or difficult work for low wages. Unless today's economies change, it is not likely that many retarded people will be employable except in unskilled, low-paying jobs. As the numbers of unemployed retarded people rise, so will the welfare rolls, leading to a possible taxpayer revolt of the kind that has begun in the United States as of this writing. The challenge for industrial society is to find some means to provide productive employment for the mentally retarded.

A final issue involves independence and the ways in which

services are typically being provided to the mentally retarded. It has often been observed that it is frequently easier for parents or for caregivers in residential facilities to do things for retarded people than it is to teach the retarded to do these things for themselves. This continues to be the case even as deinstitutionalization and normalization proceed. Parents tenaciously hold their now-adult children in dependency relationships. So do caregivers. Thus retarded people often are denied the opportunity to learn how to manage money, how to travel on buses or subways, and how to cope with the many problems that make up everyday life. Social workers and other agency personnel do the same, shielding the retarded against the dangers of normal existence. The argument is often made that the retarded have by definition proven themselves unable to cope with normal life and circumstances, but this is in fact seldom true. Most socioculturally retarded persons have proven themselves unable to cope with only one thing in life—school. Others who may have had trouble in nonschool environments have often done so because they lacked knowledge of what was appropriate, not because they lacked the ability to learn how to comport themselves in public.

Many retarded adults gladly accept the dependent role they have occupied for so long. They are more than happy to accept small loans, transportation, advice about dealings with bureaucracies, help in medical or dental appointments, shopping, handling money, reading, and the like. It is obvious that many retarded people can learn to do without help in most of these matters, but it is sometimes easier for them not to learn. Retarded adults who are learning to adapt to community living need more opportunity to learn for themselves. Clinically retarded individuals who are attempting to live normal lives may always need assistance with some aspects of their lives, and they may always need access to medical services. A system for providing that help and those services must continue to be a social priority. Socioculturally retarded persons, however, are now served by the same agencies, and most of these people are poorly served by agencies that are designed primarily to serve more severely retarded and physically handicapped people. Instead of being submitted to a panoply of agencies and personnel, socioculturally retarded people could probably become more competent and independent if they were more often allowed to solve their own problems, supported perhaps by a kind of hot-line telephone service that would quickly connect them to a knowledgeable person should they need help with a social problem or personal crisis. This recommendation derives in part from existing research with socioculturally retarded people in community settings, and in part from the fact that most socioculturally retarded individuals are able to live their lives without any help from social agencies.

Normalization is human drama of the utmost poignancy. To some extent, progress has been made, but money has been misspent and so have human lives. We all deserve better in the years ahead. But at the same time that normalization must be made to succeed, it is also essential that we attempt to understand the underlying causes of sociocultural retardation.

IQ AND SOCIOCULTURAL RETARDATION

It is only a slight exaggeration to say that the story of sociocultural retardation is the story of the IQ. In the absence of a widely accepted test of adaptive behavior, the IQ test has been —and remains—the most important criterion in determining who is and who is not mentally retarded. As we saw earlier, it is also the criterion for determining the success of early education programs, the effects of malnutrition, and so on. How has this come about?

The first formal test of "intelligence" was published in 1905 by the French psychologist Alfred Binet and his colleague Theodore Simon in response to a commission from the Minister of Public Instruction to develop a method to identify mentally retarded pupils who might be better educated in separate facilities. The test sampled a variety of mental functions having to do with judgment, comprehension, and reasoning. The first user of this test in the United States was H. H. Goddard of the Vineland Training School for retarded children. Some years later, in 1916, the IQ test was fully standardized at Stanford University by Lewis Terman. This test became known as the Stanford-Binet, and what it measured was the intelligence quotient. The IQ test has proven to be extremely accurate in doing what it was intended for—predicting which children will do badly in school and which will do well.

It is essential to keep in mind that the only thing the IQ test does is just that—it measures academic performance intelligence, not other kinds of intelligence needed for nonschool success. It does not measure musical or artistic intelligence or the ability to cope with the problems of everyday life. Furthermore, the test was standardized on the children of white English-speaking parents. It is, therefore, biased in favor of people from a white middle-class background. Although the test has utility for predicting the academic success of such children, it may do a great injustice to children who come from different cultural backgrounds. These children as a group do not score as well on IQ tests as middle-class whites do. It is true that children of Asian background (Chinese, Korean, and Japanese) do even better than middle-class white children, but on the average black, Spanish-surname, Filipino, American Indian, and poor white children score lower than the white middle-class children on whom the test was standardized.

That the test has various forms of built-in bias has long been recognized. For example, when the IQ test was being developed, it was discovered that males and females did not perform equally well. Males as a group outdid females on speed and coordination of gross motor activities, spatial problem solving, mechanical tasks, and some kinds of quantitative reasoning. Females as a group did better than males in perceptual skills, memory, fine motor skills, numerical computation, and verbal skills. Rather than develop one test standardized for males and another standardized for females, the test developers threw out test items that strongly favored either males or females and blended together just enough items that slightly favored males with some that slightly favored females, until males and females scored equally well on the test. As psychologist John Garcia has pointed out,[6] the same procedure could be employed with ethnic groups who now do poorly on the test. Items on which Chicano or black children do better than white children (and there are such items) could be blended with items that favor white children until all groups score equally well. The argument against such a procedure is that the IQ would no longer predict academic success as well as it now does. True enough, but this only underscores the basic point—IQ is not a measure of general intelligence or retardation; it is a measure of how well a child is likely to do in the existing school system.

Recognizing that IQ test scores may not correctly assess the intellectual abilities of ethnic minority children led the American Association on Mental Deficiency in 1973 to decide that the diagnosis of mental retardation can only be made if a child's IQ and adaptive behavior are *both* inadequate. Though that was certainly a step in the right direction, in practice very little has changed, since there is no test of adaptive behavior that can accurately be used with socioculturally retarded people. Adaptive behavior refers to how well a person meets the demands of a particular environment. Various efforts are underway to measure the demands made in various kinds of family environments, but there are still no means for assessing the demands of street gangs, play groups, or other environments relevant to the lives of school-age children and adults. Without reliable tests of adaptive behavior it is necessary to rely on subjective judgments. Such judgments can be entirely accurate, but they can also easily reflect the bias of the judge; as a result, most diagnosticians tend to give greater weight to the standardized IQ test.

In some parts of the United States dissatisfaction with the IQ test has been so pronounced that legislation has been proposed to prohibit the use of such tests in school systems for the purpose of diagnosing a child as mentally retarded. We cannot determine what effect such changes might have, although critics of the proposals have been quick to point out that without IQ tests it will be impossible to distinguish a high-IQ child who is having academic trouble in school from a low-IQ child having similar trouble; as a result, efforts to help either child would be sorely hampered. Be this as it may, the role of the IQ test in identifying socioculturally retarded children has been central and will probably continue to be, but the ways in which IQ test scores have been used to define mental retardation are not without arbitrariness, and this has the utmost significance for society.

Before 1959, there was general agreement among scientists in the United States that the cut-off for mental retardation would be an IQ of 75. This agreement was arbitrary; there is nothing about an IQ of 75 that identifies retarded behavior, except in

school, and there even higher IQs are associated with subaca-
demic performances. In 1973, a committee of the American Association on Mental Deficiency reduced the upper limit of retardation to 70. At this writing another committee of the
association is considering lowering the cut-off still further. Obviously, then, the limits of what is to be considered sociocultural
retardation are flexible. They could, in principle, be set anywhere. There are some important consequences that derive from
these decisions to change the upper limit of mental retardation.
First, it is essential to note that the criterion is an IQ test score.
Second, since most ethnic minority groups on the average score
lower than whites do, this means that as long as IQ is the criterion disproportionately more blacks and Chicanos, for example, will be defined as mentally retarded.

But the issues involve more than fairness or scientific pre-
cision. Adults who are identified as mentally retarded are
eligible for government support. In the United States this most
often takes the form of Supplemental Security Income, usually
in the amount of about $300 per month. When the upper limit
for mental retardation is changed, large numbers of people will
either gain or lose eligibility—and income—at a stroke of a pen,
as it were. Money for children is also involved. In 1975, the
Education for All Handicapped Children Act became law. This
law set aside $387 million for fiscal year 1977-78, to increase to
$3.1 billion by 1982. These monies will be apportioned to local
school districts and state-operated programs depending on the
identification of specific children who are eligible for services.
That identification will typically include an IQ test.

For the individuals involved and their parents, the money and
services involved can be crucial. For society, there is an inescapable issue concerning how much money taxpayers are
willing to provide, and what role a flexible IQ criterion should
play in determining who gets that money.

DOES SOCIETY CREATE MENTAL RETARDATION?

There can be little doubt that, as Lewis A. Dexter wrote some
years ago,[7] societies can and do manufacture social problems by
choosing to regard a particular sort of behavior as unacceptable.
If our schools, for example, choose to regard gawkiness (to con-

tinue Dexter's example) as a problem, then schools would have little problem identifying gawky children, placing them in special remedial classes and thereby making gawky children into problem children. And if our society did in fact emphasize grace instead of academic achievement, gawkiness would be a legitimate social problem. There is little doubt that our society, through our schools, has made sociocultural mental retardation into a greater problem than need be. If we chose to do so, we could make it into a greater problem still. This is true of mental retardation or any other social problem.

What is not clear is whether societies can "unmake" problems. Can we ignore certain categories of handicapped persons as if they were not socially problematic? Specifically, can societies choose to regard mental retardation as if it were not a social problem at all? As far as it is possible to determine, clinically retarded persons pose a problem everywhere, and even socioculturally retarded persons are a social problem in most societies, however remote, technologically backward, and nonliterate these societies may be.[8] That is so because every society makes substantial demands upon its members for competencies of all sorts—intellectual, social, and physical. Even the least complex of cultures establishes forms of proper conduct that require subtlety, self-control, tact, deceit, and verbal skill. In fact, such skills are often more highly valued in non-Western societies than they are in the West. Socioculturally retarded people in such societies often create social problems because they offend others by an inappropriate display of emotion or by a failure to observe etiquette. Every society also requires that its members live fully in time, in space, and in number. They must do so in order both to sustain creature needs and to maintain cultural values. Economic requirements are seldom simple matters either, especially among the world's more primitive, technologically deprived peoples.

In many African tribal societies, for example, economic matters are immensely complicated. A man must know the names of hundreds of cattle, their genealogical backgrounds, their personal histories, and their relative worth in a fluctuating non-money market. He must know the details of literally hundreds of economic deals involving people, animals, land, and other goods, most of which include partial and deferred payments and a bewildering number and variety of hidden contingencies. What is more, a man faces the constant dangers of war, dangerous animals, weather, crop failures, witchcraft, and supernatural malevolence. A woman must contend with a world that is no less complex and dangerous. Indeed, women must often know all that their husbands do, and then some.

As a result it is unusual to find a society anywhere that is not socially troubled by the presence of the clinically retarded among its members. Yet exactly *how* it is troubled and just *who* will be considered retarded vary greatly from society to society. In our own society, the clinically retarded have obviously always been a problem for their families, and for themselves. Since society has recognized its responsibility to assist families in caring for such people, we have all become involved, if not by our concern for the difficult, even tragic circumstances of such people, then by the necessity of paying for their welfare (in the United States, between 5 and 10 billion dollars each year).

But sociocultural retardation is a different matter. We are all incompetent at certain things—fixing broken housewares, making public speeches, controlling our children, speaking foreign languages. What is more, when we are confronted by computer technology, all but a few of us are incompetent. And so it is with many aspects of our increasingly complex way of life. As a result, at certain times and for certain kinds of intellectual activities we could *all* be judged incompetent—mentally retarded, that is. For practical purposes, this is exactly how we judge—and sometimes even label—graduate students who fail in their university studies. In graduate school, they are unable to compete, just as the socioculturally retarded cannot cope in primary school.

You might agree with this basic premise but nevertheless object to the designation "mental retardation" because all of us "normal" people possess a basic competence: there are many things that we do perfectly well, at least most of the time. But so do the socioculturally retarded. They do not read well or do mathematics well, but other things they do perfectly well. They can get a job, ride buses, stay out of trouble, enjoy television, and get along with other people. Except in school they seem to be mentally and physically able to cope with most of the demands placed upon them. As a society, we need to decide what sense it makes to call such people "mentally retarded," as if their problems and abilities were akin to those of clinically retarded persons.

Can Schools Prevent Sociocultural Retardation? We have seen that there is considerable controversy about whether schools "cause" sociocultural retardation by the way in which they identify, label, and segregate low-IQ, low-achieving children who come from poor and ethnic minority backgrounds. Although the evidence is shaky, there is reason to believe that some children whom schools identify as retarded can be "de-labeled," returned to regular classes, and expected to do just as well as other low-achieving students. These students would no longer be "mentally retarded"; they would simply be poor students.

It might be possible, then, to eliminate most sociocultural retardation in our society if schools simply failed to recognize any student as being retarded. This is a perfectly logical outcome of the fact that most socioculturally retarded children are so identified only during their years in school. But even if we delabeled such students, they would still do poorly in school and their prospects for economic success after school would continue to be below average.

Is it possible for our schools to do more than this? Can the use of preschool programs, special educational experiences, bilingual classes, or busing of minority students actually transform substantial numbers of low-IQ, low-academic performance students into average-IQ, average-performance students? Again there is controversy and we must look at both sides of the argument.

First, there is some positive evidence. In developing societies of the so-called Third World, every year that children attend formal schools improves their cognitive ability, as measured by a variety of tests including IQ tests.[9] We have already seen evidence of these improvements in performance from Das and Soysa in Sri Lanka and McKay and his colleagues in Colombia, even when the students involved were both poor and malnourished. But as we have also seen, equally clear-cut evidence that schooling itself substantially improves either IQ or academic achievement in countries which already have compulsory public education has been more difficult to find.[10]

Nevertheless, there is some evidence that carefully designed educational programs can markedly raise the academic achievement of low-IQ, low-achieving children from poor, ethnic minority backgrounds. The Milwaukee project may be one such program. Another example has been provided by psychologists Ronald Gallimore, Roland Tharp, and their colleagues in Hawaii.[11] Hawaiian children of Polynesian ancestry do not generally do well in school. Their standard third-grade achievement scores are among the lowest 10 percent recorded nationally; more specifically, most of these children do not learn to read. Gallimore, Tharp, and their associates established a primary school over which they had complete control in admissions, curriculum, and all other educational matters. The Hawaiian children admitted to this school—the Kamehameha Early Education Project (KEEP)—came from the poorest urban slum in Honolulu. Children from this same slum who attend public school do not learn to read and often drop out early. Many are thought of by school or welfare officials as mentally retarded.

When these Hawaiian children were admitted to KEEP, conventional reading programs were skillfully and diligently applied, and yet the children did not learn to read. This failure occurred despite the fact that these children were found to be extremely industrious in their school tasks; what is more, the children were found to have all the linguistic and cognitive skills thought necessary for reading. Still after three years of concerted effort they could not read. Then the researchers determined to utilize their knowledge of the culture and everyday language behavior of Hawaiian children to develop a reading program that would be consistent with the nonschool teaching and learning of the children. By tailoring their approach to the traditional Hawaiian practice of narrative storytelling, the KEEP educators were able to achieve striking gains in reading skills: these children have now been taught to read at a level that is well above the national average. Whether the methods developed at KEEP can be used to teach other ethnic minority children to improve their academic skills remains to be seen, but at least the KEEP experience suggests that important academic gains can take place under optimal educational circumstances.

Most research, however, indicates that schools can achieve only limited improvement. Indeed it has recently been shown that it is possible to predict school failure from information available at birth. The critical information about a newborn child involves birth order, education of the mother, birth weight, the month that prenatal care was begun, race, and illegitimacy.[12] When all influences on the IQ and academic achievement of children are considered, it is evident that the family environment and the peer-group culture have a far more powerful influence over school achievement than anything the schools can accomplish. Moreover, as children grow older, the influence of their homes and playmates becomes progressively more powerful. Both national and regional surveys of school achievement in the United States agree that home influences far outweigh the schools in bringing about academic achievement.[13]

Because the significance of this finding has been obscured by arguments concerning the use of IQ testing with ethnic minority children and by arguments that the lower IQs of such children are inherited, a new study from Poland takes on particular significance. This research in Warsaw by a team of Polish and American social scientists strongly reaffirmed the finding that the family is far more influential than the school in the development of mental ability and academic achievement.[14]

The city of Warsaw was almost entirely destroyed during World War II. After the war, the city was razed and rebuilt under the policies of the new socialist government, whose principle was to allocate housing, schools, and health services without regard to social class. Not only was the city rebuilt with that principle in mind; people of all classes and occupations were scattered evenly throughout the city, and subsequent migration to Warsaw was controlled as much as possible to maintain this classless society. The authors report that, in Warsaw today, people of all levels of education and all types of occupations live in apartments that closely resemble one another, shop in identical stores that contain the same goods, and share similar cultural centers. Schools and health facilities are equipped in the same way and are equally accessible. As a result, while there is still considerable socioeconomic stratification in Warsaw, with families exhibiting a range of education and occupation equivalent to that found in many non-Communist cities, these different kinds of families live in the same neighborhoods, their children attend the same schools, and they receive the same medical care.

Since the living standards are so equivalent and children of all backgrounds attend the same schools, the researchers asked whether the children would be more equivalent in IQ and academic achievement than is the case in non-Communist cities. To answer this question they studied 96 percent of the 14,238 children who were born in Warsaw in 1963 and lived in the city in 1974. These children were given an IQ test as well as various achievement tests involving arithmetic and vocabulary. Information was also collected on the age, education, occupation, and birthplace of each parent as well as the size of the family and the birth order of the children. The investigators also gathered first-hand data on the characteristics of the health services, the schools themselves, and the various neighborhoods.

The evidence demonstrated that the IQ and academic achievement of Warsaw children were very strongly related to parental education and occupation. The researchers concluded that the equalization of living conditions and schooling in Warsaw has not been able to override the circumstances of the family. Considerable differences among families in education and occupation continue to exist in Warsaw, and schooling has proven inadequate in equalizing the mental performance of Polish children. This is an extremely important finding because, while differences in education and occupation, and as a result in family microculture, exist in Warsaw, these differences cannot possibly be as profound as those found in most non-Communist cities, where there are not only great socioeconomic differences of all kinds but cultural differences among ethnic minority and poverty families as well.

Obviously it is far easier to change schools than it is to change families, neighborhoods, and cultures. But it is evident that, if truly substantial prevention of sociocultural mental retardation is to take place, that is precisely what must happen. Such an undertaking in social and cultural change is not only immensely difficult, given the social and economic conditions found in most Western cities, it is immensely complex as well. We do not yet know what it is about the family microculture of poor and ethnic minority children that we should change. Keep in mind that most children reared in such environments are *not* mentally retarded.

Necessary changes would presumably include the improvement of pre-and perinatal care so that fewer children are born prematurely or too close to one another in age, and so that mothers are well nourished, avoid drugs and alcohol, and receive good medical care. Presumably, too, we must improve the nutrition of each child and protect him from such hazards as lead, disease, and injury. But we must also change a host of subtle psychological factors having to do with the appropriateness of family and peer culture for learning. This would include such obvious factors as the motivation on the part of parents and peers for success in school, including the provision of good models for school achievement and a richly stimulating home environment. But exactly how one should provide such motivation, models, and such stimulation is something we do not know. That is why the relative failure of special educational programs cannot be regarded as proving that enriching family environment *cannot* work. To date these programs have not dealt with a sufficiently full range of factors in a child's early environment; nor have they tried hard enough to change these factors. They have equated improvement with a higher IQ score, not with improvements in adaptive behavior. Furthermore, such programs have not been continued long enough to let us determine whether the gains that have occurred can be increased or maintained.

Clearly, then, the problems of improving the family environment of children who may become retarded are many and complex. But if sociocultural retardation is to be reduced in any significant way, then we must address these many and complex aspects of a child's environment. The problem lies in this network of family factors, and so we must search for a solution there.

References
Suggested Reading
Index

References

1 What Is Mental Retardation?

1. H.J. Grossman, *A Manual on Terminology and Classification in Mental Retardation* (Washington, D.C.: American Association on Mental Deficiency, Special Publication No. 2, 1977).
2. C.E. Meyers, K. Nihira, and A. Zetlin, "The Measurement of Adaptive Behavior." In N.R. Ellis, ed., *Handbook of Mental Deficiency*, rev. ed. (New York: Lawrence Erlbaum, 1979).
3. G. Tarjan, "Some Thoughts on Socio-Cultural Retardation." In H. C. Haywood, ed., *Social-Cultural Aspects of Mental Retardation* (New York: Appleton-Century-Crofts, 1970).

2 Clinical Retardation

1. B.F. Crandall, "Genetic Disorders and Mental Retardation," *Journal of the American Academy of Child Psychiatry*, 1977, *16*, 88-108.
2. D.F. Roberts, J. Chavez, and S.D.M. Court, "The Genetic Component in Child Mortality," *Archives of Disabled Children*, 1970, *45*, 33-38.
3. K.L. Jones and D.W. Smith, "Recognition of the Fetal Alcohol Syndrome in Early Infancy," *Lancet*, 1973, *2*, 999-1101.
4. J.W. Hanson, A.P. Streissguth, and D.W. Smith, "The Effects of Moderate Alcohol Consumption During Pregnancy on Fetal Growth and Morphogenesis," *Journal of Pediatrics*, 1978, *92*, 457-460.

3 If Prevention Fails

1. J. Jacobs, *The Search for Help: A Study of the Retarded Child in the Community* (New York: Brunner-Mazel, 1969), pp. 4-5.
2. Ibid., pp. 16-17.
3. E.R. Kramm, *Families of Mongoloid Children*. Children's Bureau Publication, No. 401 (Washington, D.C.: U.S. Government Printing Office, 1963), p. 10.
4. B. Spock, *On Being a Parent of a Handicapped Child* (Chicago: National Society for Crippled Children and Adults, 1961), p. 5.
5. I.D. Todres, D. Krane, M.C. Howell, and D.C. Shannon, "Pediatricians' Attitudes Affecting Decision-Making in Defective Newborns," *Pediatricians and Ethical Dilemmas*, 1977, *60*, 197-201.

6. R.E. Magenis, et al., "Parental Origin of the Extra Chromosome in Down's Syndrome," *Human Genetics*, 1977, *37*, 7-16.
7. K. Fishler, "Mental Development in Mosaic Down's Syndrome as Compared with Trisomy 21." In R. Koch, F.F. de la Cruz, eds., *Down's Syndrome (Mongolism): Research, Prevention, and Management* (New York: Brunner-Mazel, 1975), pp. 87-98.
8. D.R. Price-Williams and S. Sobsay, "Communicative Competence among Severely Retarded Persons," *Semiotica*, in press; S. Sobsay, *Communicative Competence in Down's Syndrome Adults: A Study in the Pragmatics of Discourse and Conversation* (unpublished diss., University of California, Los Angeles, 1978).
9. N. Bayley, L. Rhodes, B. Gooch, and M. Marcus, "Environmental Factors in the Development of Institutionalized Children." In J. Hellmuth, ed., *Exceptional Infant, Vol. 2: Studies in Abnormalities* (New York: Brunner-Mazel, 1971).
10. M. V. Seagoe, *Yesterday Was Tuesday, All Night and All Day* (Boston: Little, Brown, 1964), p. 103.
11. N. Hunt, *The World of Nigel Hunt: The Diary of a Mongoloid Youth* (New York: Garrett, 1967), p. 118.
12. Ibid., pp. 125-126.

4 Caring for the Clinically Retarded

1. B. Farber and D. B. Ryckman, "Effects of Severely Retarded Children in Family Relationships," *Mental Retardation Abstracts*, 1965, *2*, 1-17.
2. K. S. Holt, "The Home Care of Severely Retarded Children," *Pediatrics*, 1958, *22*, 746-755.
3. M. S. Jackson, "Reactions of Some Australian Mothers to the Birth of Their Mentally Handicapped Child," *Slow Learning Child*, 1969, *16*, 37-43.
4. C. Hannam, *Parents and Mentally Handicapped Children.* (London: Penguin Books, 1975), p. 61.
5. J. Tizard, *Community Services for the Mentally Handicapped* (London: Oxford University Press, 1964).
6. D. J. Stedman and D. H. Eichorn, "A Comparison of the Growth and Development of Institutionalized and Home-Reared Mongoloids During Infancy and Early Childhood," *American Journal of Mental Deficiency*, 1964, *69*, 391-401.
7. P. S. Buck, *The Child Who Never Grew* (New York: John Day, 1950).
8. J. Greenfeld, in *Los Angeles Herald-Examiner*, June 12, 1978, p. 1.
9. G. Saenger, *The Adjustment of Severely Retarded Adults in the Community* (Albany: Interdepartmental Health Resources Board, 1957).

10. A. Birenbaum, and S. Seiffer, *Resettling Retarded Adults In a Managed Community* (New York: Praeger, 1976).
11. Ibid., p. xv.
12. C. Glossop, D. Felce, J. Smith, and A. Kushlick, "Comparative Evaluation of Locally-Based and 'Traditional' Hospital Units for the Mentally Handicapped in Wessex (Report No. 127, Wessex Regional Health Authority, 1977).
13. R. G. Tharp and R. J. Wetzel, *Behavior Modification in the Natural Environment*, (New York: Academic Press, 1969).
14. J. Smith, A. Kushlick, and C. Glossop, "The Wessex Portage Project: A Home Teaching Service for Families with a Pre-School Mentally Handicapped Child" (Research Report No. 125, Wessex Regional Health Authority, 1977).

5 Sociocultural Retardation

1. R. Davie, N. Butler, and H. Goldstein, *From Birth to Seven* (London: Longman and National Children's Bureau, 1972).
2. H. G. Birch, S. A. Richardson, D. Baird, G. Horobin, and R. Illsley, *Mental Subnormality in the Community: A Clinical and Epidemiological Survey* (Baltimore: Williams and Wilkins, 1970). 1970).
3. R. Gazaway, *The Longest Mile* (Garden City, New York: Doubleday, 1969).
4. Ibid., p. 53.
5. Ibid., p. 107.
6. Ibid., p. 91.
7. Ibid., p. 91.
8. Ibid., p. 83.
9. Ibid., pp. 229-30.
10. Ibid., pp. 254-55.

6 The Causes of Sociocultural Retardation

1. J. B. Watson, *Behaviorism* (Chicago: University of Chicago Press, 1925), p. 218.
2. E. Zigler, "The Nature-Nurture Issue Reconsidered." In H. C. Haywood, ed., *Social-Cultural Aspects of Mental Retardation* (New York: Appleton-Century-Crofts, 1970), p. 83.
3. J. C. Loehlin, G. Lindzey, and J. N. Spuhler, *Race Differences in Intelligence* (San Francisco: Freeman, 1975).
4. A. M. Clarke and A. D. B. Clarke, *Early Experience: Myth and Evidence* (New York: Free Press, 1976).
5. J. Kagan, "The Baby's Elastic Mind," *Human Nature*, 1978, 1, 66-73.
6. H. Garber and R. F. Heber, "The Milwaukee Project: Indications of

the Effectiveness of Early Intervention in Preventing Mental Retardation." In P. Mittler, ed. *Research to Practice in Mental Retardation: Care and Intervention*, vol. 1 (Baltimore: University Park Press, 1977).

7. R. B. Zajonc, "Family Configuration and Intelligence," *Science*, 1976, *192*, 227-292.

8. J. S. Bruner, *The Relevance of Education* (New York: Norton, 1971). B. L. White and J. Carew Watts, *Experiences and Environment: Major Influences On the Development of the Young Child* (Englewood Cliffs, N. J.: Prentice-Hall, 1973).

9. B. C. Moore and S. M. Moore, *Mental Retardation: Causes and Prevention* (Columbus, Ohio: Merrill, 1977).

10. J. J. Wesolowski, et al., "Lead in the Blood of California Children," *Western Journal of Medicine*, 1977, *127*, 271-273.

11. J. R. Hebel, D. Kinch, and E. Armstrong, "Mental Capacity of Children Exposed to Lead Pollution," *British Journal of Preventive and Social Medicine*, 1976, *30*, 170-174.

12. R. L. Boeckx, B. Postl, and F. J. Coodin, "Gasoline Sniffing and Tetraethyl Lead Poisoning in Children," *Pediatrics*, 1977, *60*, 140-145.

13. O. David, et al., "Low Lead Levels and Mental Retardation," *Lancet*, 1976, *2*, 1376-1379.

14. A. D. Beattie, M. R. Moore, A. Goldberg, et al., "Role of Chronic Low-Level Lead Exposure in the Aetiology of Mental Retardation," *Lancet*, 1975, *1*, 589; R. J. Landrigan, R. H. Whitworth, R. W. Baloh, et al., "Neuropsychological Dysfunction in Children with Chronic Low-Level Lead Absorption," *Lancet*, 1975, *1*, 708.

15. J. Dobbing, "Nutrition and the Developing Brain," *Lancet*, 1973, *1*, 48.

16. M. Winick, *Malnutrition and Brain Development* (New York: Oxford University Press, 1976).

17. M. Winick, K. K. Meyer, and R. C. Harris, "Malnutrition and Environmental Enrichment by Early Adoption," *Science*, 1975, *190*, 1173-1175.

18. J. P. Das and P. Soysa, "Late Effects of Malnutrition: A Biomedical and Psychological Study," *International Journal of Psychology*, in press.

19. H. McKay, et al., "Improving Cognitive Ability in Chronically Deprived Children," *Science*, 1978, *200*, 270-278.

20. Ibid., p. 277.

21. J. R. Mercer, *Labeling the Mentally Retarded* (Berkeley: University of California Press, 1973).

22. D. J. Franks, "Ethnic and Social Status Characteristics of Children in EMR and LD Classes," *Exceptional Children*, 1971, *37*, 537-538.

23. G. D. Broadhead, "Socioeconomic Traits in Mildly Retarded Chil-

dren of Differential Diagnosis," *Rehabilitation Literature*, 1973, *34*, 104-107.

24. D. L. MacMillan, *Mental Retardation in School and Society* (Boston: Little, Brown, 1977).

7 *After Schooling*

1. H. V. Cobb, *The Forecast of Fulfillment* (New York: Teachers College Press, 1972).
2. E. M. Gruenberg, "Epidemiology." In H. A. Stevens and R. F. Heber, eds. *Mental Retardation: A Review of Research* (Chicago: University of Chicago Press, 1964).
3. W. R. Baller, D. C. Charles, and E. L. Miller, "Mid-Life Attainment of the Mentally Retarded," *Genetic Psychology Monographs*, 1967, *75*, 235-329.
4. Ibid., p. 87.
5. A. M. Henshel, *The Forgotten Ones: A Sociological Study of Anglo and Chicano Retardates* (Austin: University of Texas Press, 1972).
6. S. A. Richardson, "Carers of Mentally Retarded Young Persons: Services, Jobs, and Interpersonal Relations," *American Journal of Mental Deficiency*, 1978, *82*, 349-358.
7. J. Mattinson, *Marriage and Mental Handicap* (London: Duckworth, 1970).
8. N. M. Robinson and H. B. Robinson, *The Mentally Retarded Child: A Psychological Approach*, 2nd ed. (New York: McGraw-Hill, 1976).
9. R. B. Edgerton, *The Cloak of Competence* (Berkeley: University of California Press, 1967).
10. Ibid., p. 204.
11. S. Olshansky, "Changing Vocational Behavior Through Normalization." In Wolfensberger, ed., *Normalization: The Principle of Normalization in Human Services* (Toronto: Leonard Crainford, 1972), p. 159.
12. R. B. Edgerton and S. Bercovici, "The Cloak of Competence— Years Later," *American Journal of Mental Deficiency*, 1976, *80*, 485-497.
13. S. Terkel, *Working: People Talk about What They Do All Day and How They Feel about What They Do* (New York: Random House, 1972).
14. R. B. Edgerton and L. L. Langness, "Observing Mentally Retarded Persons in Community Settings: An Anthropological Perspective." In G. D. Sackett, ed., *Observing Behavior, Vol. I: Theory and Applications in Mental Retardation* (Baltimore: University Park Press, 1978).

8 Some Implications for Society

1. A. W. Butler, "The Feeble-Minded: The Need for Research," *Proceedings of the National Conference on Charities and Correction,* 1915, p. 361.
2. W. N. Bullard, "State Care of High-Grade Imbecile Girls," *Proceedings of the National Conference on Charities and Correction,* 1910, p. 302.
3. W. E. Fernald, "Care of the Feeble-Minded," *Proceedings of the National Conference on Charities and Correction,* 1904, p. 383.
4. "The Goal Is Freedom," *President's Committee on Mental Retardation* (Washington, D. C.: Department of Health, Education and Welfare, 1973), p. 24.
5. S. J. Vitello, "Beyond Deinstitutionalization: What's Happening to the People?" *Amicus,* 1977, 40-44.
6. J. Garcia, "IQ: The Conspiracy," *Psychology Today,* 1972, *6,* 40-43, 92-93.
7. L. A. Dexter, *The Tyranny of Schooling: An Inquiry into the Problem of "Stupidity"* (New York: Basic Books, 1964).
8. R. B. Edgerton, "Mental Retardation in Non-Western Societies: Toward a Cross-Cultural Perspective on Incompetence." In H. C. Haywood, ed., *Social-Cultural Aspects of Mental Retardation* (New York: Appleton-Century-Crofts, 1970).
9. M. Cole and S. Scribner, *Culture and Thought: A Psychological Introduction* (New York: Wiley, 1974).
10. J. C. Leohlin, G. Lindzey, and J. N. Spuhler, *Race Differences in Intelligence* (San Francisco: Freeman, 1975).
11. C. Jordan, et al., "A Multidisciplinary Approach to Research in Education: The Kamehameha Early Education Program." Paper at the annual meeting of the American Anthropological Association, Houston, December 1977.
12. C. T. Ramey, D. J. Stedman, A. Borders-Patterson, and W. Mengal, "Predicting School Failure from Information Available at Birth," *American Journal of Mental Deficiency,* 1978, *82,* 525-534.
13. J. S. Coleman, et al., *Equality of Educational Opportunity* (Washington, D.C.: U.S. Office of Education, 1966). C. Jencks, et al., *Inequality: A Reassessment of the Effect of Family and Schooling In America* (New York: Basic Books, 1972).
14. A. Firkowska, et al., "Cognitive Development: The Contribution of Parental Occupation and Education to Mental Performance in 11-Year-Olds in Warsaw," *Science,* 1978, *200,* 1357-1362.

Suggested Reading

Michael J. Begab and Stephen A. Richardson, eds., *The Mentally Retarded and Society: A Social Science Perspective* (Baltimore: University Park Press, 1975). A stimulating selection of papers, for professionals as well as general readers.

Felix de la Cruz and Gerald D. LaVeck, eds., *Human Sexuality and the Mentally Retarded: Some Sociocultural Research Considerations* (New York: Brunner-Mazel, 1973). Probably the best available survey of the subject.

Richard Koch and Felix de la Cruz, eds., *Down's Syndrome (Mongolism): Research, Prevention and Management* (New York: Brunner-Mazel, 1975). Topics include causes, prenatal detection, developmental progress, possible therapies, early environmental intervention, language, and community adaptation.

H. Carl Haywood, ed., *Social-Cultural Aspects of Mental Retardation* (New York: Appleton-Century-Crofts, 1970). Although almost ten years old, these discussions of mental retardation are among the best ever published. Any serious student of the field should read this book.

Donald L. MacMillan, *Mental Retardation in School and Society* (Boston: Little, Brown, 1977). An up-to-date, well-balanced review of the social context of mental retardation; the treatment of special education and schooling in general is especially good.

Jane R. Mercer, *Labeling the Mentally Retarded* (Berkeley: University of California Press, 1973). An important contribution to our understanding of how members of ethnic minority populations become labeled mentally retarded.

Byron C. Moore and Susan M. Moore, *Mental Retardation: Causes and Prevention* (Columbus, Ohio: Merrill, 1977). A readable, nontechnical introduction, with emphasis on clinical retardation.

Wolf Wolfensberger, *The Principle of Normalization in Human Service* (Toronto: National Institute of Mental Retardation, 1972). A classic statement of the history and philosophy of normalization; also contains specialized discussions, including the role of employment and the "dignity of risk."

Index